TO HELL WITH THE HUSTLE

PRAISE FOR
TO HELL WITH THE HUSTLE

"My friend Jefferson Bethke is brilliant and he is modeling in his life and family what he is writing in these pages and it is working. It is inspiring and convicting to watch someone flourish as they let go when culture hangs on and rest when culture says to run. To live like Jesus, to work and rest like Jesus, is the desire of so many hearts (mine included), and Jeff is leading us toward that life."

—Annie F. Downs, bestselling author of *100 Days to Brave* and host of the *That Sounds Fun* podcast

"Ever feel like you need to work harder, put in more time to get ahead, or do everything in your power to be the best? That's the hustle. It can push you to places you don't want to go, and I've gone there more than I care to admit. In his latest book, *To Hell with the Hustle*, Jefferson Bethke will help you understand why the hustle can seem so alluring, show you how to avoid the traps it's created in our culture, and find true joy chasing after Christ instead."

—Craig Groeschel, pastor of Life.Church and *New York Times* bestselling author

"If anyone can speak to the topic of removing 'hustle' from our vocabulary, it would be Jefferson. I've watched him practice what he preaches on this, so the words in this book do not come without testing. This book will challenge you to live a life that relies on God."

—Jennie Allen, author of *Nothing to Prove*, founder and visionary of IF:Gathering

"*To Hell with the Hustle* is just the prescription we need in our hustle culture. Everybody is hustling, but what are we really accomplishing? What toll is the hustle having on our souls? Read this book. Jeff will teach you the better way to find the life you are looking for."

—Dr. Derwin L. Gray, author of *Limitless Life: You Are More than Your Past When God Holds Your Future*

TO HELL WITH THE HUSTLE

RECLAIMING YOUR LIFE IN AN OVERWORKED, OVERSPENT, AND OVERCONNECTED WORLD

JEFFERSON BETHKE

NELSON
BOOKS

An Imprint of Thomas Nelson

Published in Nashville, Tennessee, by Nelson Books, an imprint of Thomas Nelson. Nelson Books and Thomas Nelson are registered trademarks of HarperCollins Christian Publishing, Inc.

Published in association with Yates & Yates, www.yates2.com.

Thomas Nelson titles may be purchased in bulk for educational, business, fund-raising, or sales promotional use. For information, please e-mail SpecialMarkets@ThomasNelson.com.

Unless otherwise noted, Scripture quotations are taken from the Holy Bible, New International Version˚, NIV˚. Copyright © 1973, 1978, 1984, 2011 by Biblica, Inc.˚ Used by permission of Zondervan. All rights reserved worldwide. www.Zondervan.com. The "NIV" and "New International Version" are trademarks registered in the United States Patent and Trademark Office by Biblica, Inc.˚

Scripture quotations marked ESV are from the ESV˚ Bible (The Holy Bible, English Standard Version˚). Copyright © 2001 by Crossway, a publishing ministry of Good News Publishers. Used by permission. All rights reserved.

Any Internet addresses, phone numbers, or company or product information printed in this book are offered as a resource and are not intended in any way to be or to imply an endorsement by Thomas Nelson, nor does Thomas Nelson vouch for the existence, content, or services of these sites, phone numbers, companies, or products beyond the life of this book.

ISBN 978-0-7180-3921-9 (eBook)
ISBN 978-0-7180-3920-2 (TP)

Library of Congress Control Number:2019947270

Printed in the United States of America
HB 02.11.2020

To Lucy, Kannon, and Kinsley
I pray the way of Jesus continues to become your highest
pursuit and ultimate treasure as you grow day by day.
Love, Dad

CONTENTS

A TIME TO RESIST

We were both on the couch. She was crying. Then I heard, "You should've married someone else!"

I stood and started pacing. "Are you *serious* right now?!" It's a question that has never helped a single marital situation since the dawn of humanity.

It's a tough thing to hear your wife say she wishes you had married someone else. It's even tougher when, for a second, you think she might be right.

We wouldn't be in this situation if I had.

But I didn't *want* to marry anyone else. I believe Alyssa is God's gift and a physical representation of grace to me. In that moment, though, it sure felt like life would have been easier if I had married someone a little bit more like me. Why did she have to be so different? Nonetheless, here we were, married for four years, with a two-year-old and an infant sleeping in the other room, feeling like our lives were burdening us and weighing us down.

Over and over again, we'd been facing the same issue. When it came to making decisions about work and future commitments, we'd clash. This was exacerbated by both of us being depleted and overwhelmed most of the time. Parenting toddlers, being self-employed, and still needing to feed ourselves three times a day were more than enough to keep track of without a deep, recurring marital conflict thrown into the mix. Here was the crux of it: when I'm over-whelmed, burned out, and tired, my default position is "let's go," while Alyssa's is "let's stop." At those times, I don't tend to give anything thoughtful consideration because I'm running on empty. I'm too exhausted for decision-making so I just say yes. Alyssa is the opposite. When she is burning out she gets anxious, and to avoid feeling crushed or over-whelmed she automatically says no to any new demands. So for the first few years of our marriage, I felt like she was holding me back, and she felt like I was bulldozing her with all my ideas and dreams and my fast pace. I felt con-fused because I thought we were doing everything we were supposed to be doing. We got married, had kids, got jobs, and worked hard—all the seemingly appropriate cultural milestones done at the culturally appropriate times (mar-ried at twenty-three, had kids at twenty-five, had jobs that were meaningful and enjoyable by twenty-two, and were homeowners by twenty-five). We went to church every week. We read our Bibles and prayed. We were doing all the right things, but we sure didn't *feel* like we were. Instead of experiencing fulfillment and happiness, we were tired, wired, anxious, and on edge.

Why did it feel like what we thought we were supposed to be doing was the very thing causing this disillusionment?

It was as if we were trying to build a life on the moon. If you've seen that famous video of Neil Armstrong landing on the moon, you know that when you are on the moon, you're ungrounded. There's no gravity holding you down. You kind of just float around—and the danger is, if you aren't tethered to anything, you'll float off into space indefinitely.

We as humans aren't meant to float off into space. We are meant to live with our feet on the ground, so to speak. To be attached and connected to something that can anchor us in the dirt.

But because of unrealistic expectations, most of us are building our lives and families on the moon, and we're floating off into space without realizing it.

After only a decade or two of living up to these cultural expectations, many of us turn around and realize we can't find the meaning we thought we were striving for. We've been hustling, but hustling toward an empty grave. Lifeless. Less human. Because we're busier. More frantic. More disconnected. Lonelier.

But what if hustle is actually what got us to this point?[1] What if it's not the solution, but the problem? What if hustle is a contagion that is flowing through our veins in subtle, under-the-surface ways? Sooner or later, we will see symptoms.

In fact, I think we are starting to.

But let's back up.

Within the last hundred or so years, we have made incredible strides in production and labor-saving devices; and at first, the breakthroughs were so enormous that people couldn't envision what we would do with all the "free time" we would be creating for ourselves. Economist John Keynes said in 1915, "For the first time since his creation man will be faced with his real, his permanent problem," and that is "how to occupy the leisure."[2]

Am I the only one who will say that my main problem in life is *not* "how to occupy the leisure"? In fact, I say, *What leisure?*

Keynes was vastly wrong. That's not what happened. In an article highlighting these developments, Derek Thompson noted one large change no one saw coming: how work itself and our view of it evolved. Work jumped from being a means of "material production" to being much more about "identity production."[3] In other words, work used to be about making things. Then all of a sudden, work was about making *us*.

We began to view our work as our reason for living, our purpose. A recent Gallup poll concluded that very thing: "Like all employees, millennials care about their income. But for this generation, a job is about more than a paycheck—it's about a purpose."[4]

When our work becomes who we are and we derive

our ultimate value and meaning from it, it runs the risk of becoming our god. The thing we worship. Bow down to. Become slaves of.

And that's what they didn't foresee a hundred years ago. That we would actually find our very center and being in *the hustle itself.*

We'd find it while we're busy finding "our passion."

While we're trying to lifehack our way through life.

While leaving or bucking off anything that is uncomfortable, unpalatable, or unenjoyable, because the hustle and our passion should never feel that way, right?

When something is our god, we will give our all for it. We will sacrifice everything.

It's no coincidence that Americans "work longer hours, have shorter vacations, get less in unemployment, disability, and retirement benefits, and retire later, than people in comparably rich societies," as Samuel P. Huntington wrote.[5]

And a recent Pew Research report on the epidemic of youth anxiety noted that 95 percent (yes, you read that right, virtually every single person who participated) said that "having a job or career they enjoy would be 'extremely or very important' to them as an adult."[6] It is *the* very thing we are all running toward to give us meaning. To give us life. To tell us *we matter.*

Not to mention this is even more pronounced by the impossibly high standards we set for our dreams and goals and work. Every person in my generation (millennials) is expected to not only have a job but also have one that is cool, is fulfilling, and reflects well on us. As Anne Petersen noted in her brilliant, recent piece titled "How Millennials Became the Burnout Generation," we think we "need to find employment that reflects well on our parents . . . that's also impressive to our peers," and that fulfills us.[7] But, Petersen continued, the problem with thinking *"Your dream job is out there, so never stop hustling—*is that it's a blueprint for spiritual and physical exhaustion."[8]

It seems others are seeing the same thing. Hustle is being put on notice. As it should be.

The research is clear:

- 7 in 10 millennials would say they are currently experiencing some level of burnout.[9]
- 54 percent of us (millennials) would say we are chronically lonely and say that we "always or sometimes feel that no one knows [us] well."[10]
- 30 percent of millennials and Gen Z currently say they experience disruptive anxiety or depression.[11]

The pressure is too much. It's unrealistic. And it's hurting us. We are paralyzed while trying to keep up. To hell with being anxious, lonely, and burned out. This isn't God's design. We are meant to flourish by the Spirit of God under the reign and rule of our King Jesus. Does this mean we won't be anxious ever? That we'll never be lonely? Never be tired? Of course not. But we are children of the King and more than conquerors[12] and we have every spiritual blessing in the heavenly places.[13] Do we believe—at least a little—that our lives would change if we fully embraced those truths and let them have actual weight in our lives? I think so.

And this isn't just our personal anxieties; it's our culture and our generation at large.

It's as if millions of us are on a treadmill, believing we're going somewhere when we're actually going nowhere. All that work, energy, and effort—yet we're running for nothing. Even worse, it feels like someone is pushing the up arrow on the treadmill constantly so we have to run faster and faster just to stay on.

Yet, I think it's a treadmill none of us wants to be on.

Something about our culture has hypnotized us. It's *alluring*, and it sucks us into the vortex with its immense influence.

It's not unlike the story of the frog and the water. If you put a frog in water that is already boiling, it will jump right out from the sheer pain and collision of senses. But if you put a frog in water at room temperature, then steadily raise the heat one degree at a time until it is boiling, the frog will slowly but eventually die.

Our culture—us—we're that frog right now, thinking, *This is nice and cozy*, but the heat has been climbing. This book is me saying, *Wait a minute. It's starting to get a little warm in here.* The values and pace of our culture, the speed at which it is moving, the demands and pressure we all collectively feel, the ethos of hustle injected into us all at birth—it's all boiling us alive. But we don't notice it because it has happened steadily over the last century or so.

It's time to stop and consider the cost of all of this hustle. All this speed. All this disillusionment. And just like most antidotes, I think a better way forward comes in administering the very opposite of the disease. We are slowly crushing our souls with noise, fame, work, and tribalism; we're living in our own private hells that are dragging us down spiritually, emotionally, and physically. So I say to hell with the hustle. And I mean that in *two ways*. To hell with it, meaning I'm done. Full stop. We can defiantly say no to where this is all headed. And two, I also truly mean *to hell with it*. Jesus was never in a hurry. Jesus was the fully human one. The prototype of all humanity. And I think we can pretty easily see that he was someone actively resisting cultural pressures, on many levels. Hustle isn't him. And if hustle isn't him, there's only one other place it could come from. Hell. The curse. The source of death.

I am realizing that only those who are anchored in a richer and deeper and more meaningful experience than the one our culture is currently offering won't get sucked away.

So what is this book about? It's about the disease, but mainly about the cure. It's about silence, obscurity, rest, and empathy—the things that make us deeply and profoundly human. And we'd do well to hold on to them during a time when no one else is.

Because, in truth, *I'm over it.*

I'm over us being statistically the most anxious and depressed generation in history.

I'm over friends by the dozens struggling to find any sense of purpose or meaning.

I'm over people destroying their lives, relationships, and marriages on the altar of working themselves to death.

And I'm over simply living in a society where franticness and a tornado of the soul are the norms.

What you're reading right now is me putting my fist in the air and saying no. I'm done. I will not take one step further down this path. I refuse to glorify and elevate the grind, the hashtag #nosleepmovement, the noise, and the commodification of our personhood through these little rectangular glass devices in our pockets.

Who's with me?

1.

WE'RE BEING FORMED,

WHETHER WE LIKE IT OR NOT

If a whiteboard were a love language, it would be mine. Who cares about "quality time" or acts of service?[1] I just want to brainstorm and scribble about ideas.

While I love to use the whiteboard for just about anything, it also shows up in a few predictable and big ways for our family at the end of every year during our Bethke Family Summit. This is a fun practice we started a few years ago where we carve out a few days at the end of every December to reflect on the past year, cast vision for the coming year, and check in on how we are doing in areas like growing together, parenting the kids, and more. On the first year of our summit, Alyssa and I had a nice dinner away from the kids, and with a blank journal nearby, we started asking and answering questions. It has evolved and grown into a multi-day super fun and celebratory reflection camp that includes our toddler-aged kids. It's like a corporate team-building event plus a vision-casting retreat, yet just for our little family team, and when they're older, we'll incorporate our kids' input too.

But here's one thing that might surprise you. One of our rules for the summit is *no talking about goals.* We aren't allowed to talk about or even use the language of "goals." We spend a few days reflecting and dreaming and connecting about the past year and the one coming up, and we don't even set one goal.

Why?

There's a principle in financial investing called a *stop-loss order.* It's essentially a benchmark set to automatically get rid of a stock if it drops below a certain value. If you buy a stock for fifty dollars, then you could set a stop-loss order for thirty dollars. So if the stock dips to thirty dollars, it'd automatically be sold in the system without you actively doing it.

A few years ago, Alyssa and I looked at each other and knew that we had reached our stop-loss order for goals. The results we were getting from the goals we were setting had dipped far below what we wanted to get back from them. So we sold it back into the system. Moved on. We haven't set goals since. And here's why: for our family, goals haven't really helped us become who we want to be.

So we swapped them with one word: *formations*, which is the "process of forming."

What's the difference? Keep in mind the definition of a *goal*: "the object of a person's ambition or effort; an aim or desired result." You can already see a stark difference between a goal and formation just in their definitions.

One is about the end. The other is about the present.
One is about doing. The other is about being.
One is about results. The other is about process.

To me they are similar, but the word *formations* seems to capture a bigger, truer idea. Goals are about *what practices I'm doing*. Formations are, too, but because they *add* a few extra words in the beginning, they take on a deeper layer: formations are *who I am becoming through the practices I'm doing*. While this has been a tiny and perhaps a semantic change, it has yielded a massive difference in our lives. It has shifted our north star so we see ourselves through not what we achieve but who we are becoming, and we are putting tiny, micro, and repeatable practices in our path that will take us there.

In short, how we live forms us into a particular human. And we have to ask, is that the same human Jesus envisioned for our flourishing and our lives?

I think if we were honest, most of us would answer no.

I'll even say it a little more plainly for those in the back: we as humans are the summation of our repeated practices and rituals. Humans aren't made. We are *formed*.

So Alyssa and I over the last few years have leaned into this forming idea, asking ourselves, Who are we becoming through the practices we are doing? And, can we create or point ourselves toward certain practices that make us the fuller, richer, more anchored humans we are meant to be? And this matters. For a few reasons. One, it feels more human. We are designed and primarily wired for becoming, not achieving. And two, I think in Christian circles we tend to focus far too much on assessing every decision we make through a lens of morality—is it right or is it wrong? There is merit to this, but I think it's too simple. It's elementary. And it doesn't take us where we need to go ultimately. It's why a Christian may not be doing anything morally "wrong," yet is addicted to being busy, feeling frantic, and overall staying anxious in their work and relationships, which clearly doesn't line up with the way of Jesus. To follow Jesus we need to not just follow his teaching, but also follow his way. His process. His cadence. His demeanor. His spirit. His very essence.

Who am I becoming through the practices I'm doing?

That's the better and truer question.

A couple of the small changes Alyssa and I have pursued are honoring a family sabbath, never allowing phones in the bedrooms, and turning off our phones once a week for a twenty-four-hour period. They have yielded massive results. And guess what? There's no finish line on them. They aren't goals. We aren't trying to do them for a month or a year or only do them one hundred times and then take them off the list. We are committed to consistently and constantly coming back to these repeatable behaviors over decades, knowing they are forming and making us into people we want to become. Becoming like Jesus is the one and only "goal" we have. (I also am fully aware that sounds a little cliché and corny, but it has shifted and changed our behavior by pointing all of our formation toward the true north of intimacy with Jesus.) We're not just doing a bunch of things. We're leaning on our very practices to take us there. To *form* us.

But first let's chat about where our cultural practices are currently taking us before we chat about where they *should* be taking us.

Information Is Killing Us

We have access to an unprecedented amount of information. We can essentially read, watch, look up, and listen to just about *anything at any time.*

We also care more about and do more with that information than ever before. I don't think we can even envision a farmer in 1803 spending copious amounts of time counting his calories or doing some new coconut oil lifehack for the longevity of his skin.

We are focused on trying to be better than ever. We have more goal-setting tools and more tips and tricks to help us become faster, better, stronger. But at what point do we pause and ask the obvious question: With all this authority and knowledge and enhancement to our personal lives, why aren't we immensely better for it? Why are we maybe even worse because of it? Essentially, why aren't we superhuman yet?

Maybe it's because we aren't supposed to be.

To the many lifehackers out there who are trying to optimize their bodies and health and minds, thinking that somehow they will unlock the key to life by doing so, I ask: Have you ever taken an honest look at the human body to see how ridiculously inefficient and gross it actually is? It doesn't matter what new biohacking diet we are on; we still expel waste out of our bodies *every single day. We are literally waste-creating devices.* And if we don't shower or put on some type of deodorant we begin to smell. Quickly. We aren't shiny machines trying to get newer and better software updates. We are earthen vessels of dust with the very Spirit of God in us.

While we're busy trying out the latest productivity system, at the end of the day we still need to sleep eight hours. Imagine if Apple tried to sell you a computer and they advertised it by saying, "This computer is inoperable for eight hours a day."

Have you ever reconciled the fact that if you live to ninety, you will have slept for thirty full years of your life? An entire thirty years with your eyes closed, not engaged in the world, not even awake and certainly not doing anything the world deems productive.

Maybe it would do us good to actually ponder the age-old wisdom, "All come from dust, and to dust all return" (Eccl. 3:20). Our bodies are filthy, gross, smelly, and decaying. But before we get too down on ourselves, let's remember that when God wanted to enter our story, how did he do it? By wrapping himself in one of those very same bodies. Forever holy. Forever glorified.

So how many bulletproof coffees do we have to drink before we actually start becoming the person we want to become? How many bullet journals do we have to crack open, podcasts do we have to listen to, Whole30 initiatives do we have to start, before we can be finished?

The truth is, we are informationally obese. Gorging ourselves on information until we are sick and unhealthy. Just one more podcast, one more YouTube video, one more hack to achieve a more optimized life.

But we keep wondering, *Why isn't anything changing?* Why do we achieve a goal or a dream yet still feel as unfilled and anxious as ever?

Was a tentmaker in the first century or a farmer in the

seventeenth century really worse off because they didn't know how to go from *Good to Great* or they weren't sure of the *Seven Habits of Highly Effective People*? (Both are good books, by the way.) Or maybe they knew something we didn't. Maybe they *didn't* know everything we know and that was actually the blessing. On average, people two hundred years ago were lucky to read fifty books in their entire lifetime. Today, people spend more time watching episodes or movies, and they watch more than fifty,[2] sometimes just in a week or two. The information onslaught is an intense issue that we haven't dealt with before.

Not all information is bad, of course. Helpful tips about ways to live better have blessed many, myself included. I, too, have found little tips online that have helped my focus and energy. What if we are attempting to exchange wisdom for shortcuts? One requires years of life experiences, while the other simply requires a Google search. Today, we face a huge gap between who we are and who we want to be simply because we can actually see that gap better than ever before. By just opening Instagram or reading Facebook posts, we see a different, perhaps ideal, self we wish we were.

Call it gorging on information. Call it getting drunk on information. Call it information abuse or addiction. Whatever you call it, it's killing us, and it's doing it silently. And I say give or take about eighty years before there will be a strong cultural consensus saying, *Yeah, this isn't what we thought it was.*

Let's not forget that cocaine was considered a wonder drug a hundred years ago and companies put it in butter and wine and soda. It was even marketed as helpful for curing stomachaches and depression.

In the 1930s and 1940s, even after tobacco companies started to realize their product was harmful and causing people to die, they didn't shut down or change. No, they paid millions of dollars to hire PR firms to convince doctors to smoke cigarettes, believing that if they could show the world that doctors were okay with smoking, then regular people would be too.

I have to wonder, are social media and Google the tobacco companies of the twenty-first century? Are smart-phones the cocaine of today? After all, our society has long had a pattern of considering something new as invigorating and exciting, adopting it at full scale and with full embrace without questioning the consequences. Then, thirty or fifty years later, the negative impact begins to show, and regulations start to pop up.

Sadly, innovation always outpaces regulation. The cycle is the same. It usually goes a little something like this:

1. This is cool and exciting.
2. This is actually the best thing ever created. How did people even live without it before?
3. This is still the best thing ever, and I can't imagine my life without it, but it seems to be hurting me also.

4. Ah yes, it's definitely hurting me, and I probably need to live without it in some way. Let's make a few rules to help us out.

As a society, I'd say we are currently in number two, with a few people starting to recognize and live into number three, which means we still have a long way to go until there are appropriate boundaries and maybe even government intervention—in 2050.

Here are a few insane flyovers to describe just *how much information* we are talking about:

- Five quintillion bytes of data is created every day.[3]
- Only 0.5 percent of all data is ever analyzed or used.[4]
- Every two days we develop as much information as we did between the dawn of civilization and 2003.[5]
- By 2020, 1.7 megabytes of new information will be created every second for every human being on the earth.[6]

To think that in just forty-eight hours, the amount of information and data produced in the world will have been equal to all the information from the beginning of time until the turn of the century is unbelievable. That means the actual amount of data we consume in a day would have been one person's entire lifetime's worth in 1574.

We are fat and drunk on information. Stumbling

through our lives. Except this abuse is the most culturally accepted in the history of mankind. In fact, we don't even recognize there is a problem yet. We are all "data junkies living in a data junkyard,"[7] as one author put it. The more we consume information and the more we keep our faces in front of the water hose of the Internet, the more we lose the very skills needed to say no to it in the first place—we lose a long, steady focus and a deep flow for work. This is probably why ten years ago you'd read for three hours at a time but now you can only go for ten minutes before checking text messages.

With all this data and information, we are more obsessed with metrics and goals than ever, but our *telos* (which is Greek for "ultimate end or aim")—our vision of the good life—doesn't seem to be becoming a reality.

But let's pause there for a second. The word *telos* is really important to this discussion. We don't have a modern English equivalent of the word, but our telos is that picture we all hold in our minds of *that's where I want to go, that's who I want to be, and that's how I want it to look when I get there.*

And whether we realize it or not, our telos is our most primal defining feature. We will bend and break an entire life around what we believe our telos to be.

And this is why it's specifically important to enter the conversation around information and data. We lean into information because we believe it's going to give us a certain future (our telos). But how's that going for us? When are we going to realize it's not taking us where we want to go?

The bottom line is, we can't research or *think* ourselves to a better version of ourselves. And this has to be reckoned with. We are not computers just waiting for a data offload or software update. In fact, we are more creaturely than we think. More primal. More animalistic. And while those drives and desires in us can be bent toward things that are evil or unhealthy, we have to remember that we were creatures before the curse as well. In other words, our impulses and desires and drives are part of what it means to be human (and pointing those desires or drives or impulses in the wrong direction is what it means to not be human).

We do not become just what we think. We become what we *desire*.

We are not shaped by facts. We are shaped by what we love.

Goals Are Finite and Final

The term *goals* was virtually nonexistent before 1920. On a graph, looking at any mention of the word in all of literature across the board, it's pretty much a flat line—until 1920, when it started to uptick and has continued to shoot up and to the right for the past ninety to one hundred years.[8]

Yet generations before us built countries without

goal-setting. Electricity and the lightbulb were invented without bullet journals. New modes of transportation like the locomotive train, and the cross-country tracks that allowed unheard-of travel across the new frontier, were created without New Year's resolutions. It makes me feel bad for Alexander Hamilton or Mozart—if only they would've known about goal-setting.

Here's the bitter truth: a lot of people have the same goals, but not a lot of people reach them. If you asked an NBA player what his goal was, he would probably say, to win a championship. The winners and losers always have the same goals. But they don't always have the same *systems*.

When I look back at my old journals, I laugh at how ridiculous and naive and uninformed I used to be. But right after I stop laughing, I'm struck with fear, wondering if I will look back at myself in five years and think the same thing.

Probably.

That's how growth as humans works.

A few years ago, my goals included:

- Eat better.
- Write a book.
- Read my Bible every day.
- Get an A in my philosophy class.

I'd then set actionable steps to try to achieve each one, usually with a benchmark of my ideal reality. I wanted to eat better so I could have six-pack abs. I wanted to write a book so I could say I was a published author. I wanted to read my Bible every day so I could become a better Christian.

But then I started running into walls.

Most of my goals—especially the big, yearly ones I'd start on New Year's Day—would last until February, and then I'd completely abandon or forget them. Because the hard truth is, finish lines and end-result motivators do not change us. They usually feel too daunting or too disconnected from our current, everyday lives. And most people don't thrive under the pressure that we heap on ourselves to hit an exact bull's-eye, not to mention that we feel ashamed if we miss it.

We need to stop thinking, *I'm not that awesome or good enough right now, but if I can just do this one thing, then maybe I'll feel better about myself.* The idea that somehow the achievement of a goal will make us a certain type of person and that it will immediately rid us of our current unhappiness and discontentment just isn't true.

I've begun to understand that we are created for formation, not goal-setting. In general, goals are usually about a finish line. Something you can reach for and then be done once you accomplish it. It's about doing something. Formations, on the other hand, aren't about doing *something* but about being *someone.* One is usually about activity, while the other is about identity. Goals are linear and resemble a straight line. Formations look more like a circle, where you are constantly coming back to the same place to seek renewal and refreshment in a particular practice. One is about a result; the other is about a process.

Some people, when they begin a new hobby, get a huge burst of ambition. Take running, for example. They'll almost immediately tell themselves, *I want to run a 10K or half marathon by this time next year.* That's helpful and great. But I think a better approach is to focus on identity: *I want to be someone who runs as a normal part of my life.* Or, *I will run at least five minutes five days a week.*

There's no finish line. Nothing to really accomplish. Make it more of a practice or way of life that will hopefully stay with you for the next sixty years. Because it's not about the marathon. It's about *I'm a runner.* And the latter to me seems to bring longer, deeper, richer benefits.

And why does this distinction matter so much? I think because Scripture doesn't talk much about goals. But it is deeply focused on our identity. On who we are becoming.

Are we becoming more like Jesus by the practices and formations we are doing?

Another important difference is the 80 percent rule. If you set goals and only do them 80 percent of the time (like working out, for example), you very quickly feel like a failure. You only think of the 20 percent of the time you didn't meet your own expectations. But with formations, if you are doing it 80 percent of the time, you can still very much know that the rhythm is changing your quality of life and who you are fundamentally. Why? Because formations are about the process itself. The process is what makes you who you are. If I'm watering our plants five days of the week instead of seven, those are still going to be awesome, healthy plants. Or if Alyssa and I try to have a rhythm of a weekly date night but only seem to do three a month for a season, we know it's helping and connecting us in ways that are very much necessary.

Here's a quick way to think about it. Traditional goals are like an arrow aiming for a bull's-eye. Formations, though, are less like a bull's-eye and more like an arrow bent in a circle.

One is linear and final. One is circular and forever.

One doesn't really change you. One can transform your life.

It's a subtle difference, but what's beautiful about formations is you get both—the process of becoming and probably the achievement or "finish line" too.

Goals tend to have a six-month lifespan, while formations you decide on usually weekly or daily for a long, possibly indefinite, amount of time. That's because formations are about becoming someone and not doing something. It's about becoming someone through the daily rhythms and practices of your life.

Who Are You Today?

Think of yourself at your current stage in life. Your job, your romantic interests, your self-development. Now think back two years. Would the you of two years ago be happy or excited with how the last two years panned out in relation to your goals and plans and dreams? When I encourage people to ask themselves that question, the answer is sometimes no. They've ended up in a slightly different place than they were planning.

That's usually because they wanted their *beliefs* (which includes hopes and dreams about themselves) to get them where they wanted to go. But I don't know one person who could simply think themselves into transformation or a life change. Do you?

So then, what gets us to where we want to go?

You probably think I'll say being disciplined. Or trying harder. Or having a little more willpower. And while all that's partially true, I think it's misleading. (Actually that's the thing that most bothers me about all the self-help and business leadership books currently—just hustle and work harder and *then* you can reach your dreams and have the life you want. *Cringe.*)

Here's the peculiar truth—what forms our identities are the million, tiny, micro-sized actions we all do every day without realizing it or thinking twice about it.

We are the sum of our habits.

It's really that simple.

Now if you ask yourself the question above, I bet you can backtrack your last few years and say, *Yeah, my daily ritualistic behaviors are usually second nature, and they have taken me in a particular direction.*

Here's the thing about habits: they are less about *doing* something and more about *loving* something. We sleep with our phones right by our bed, sometimes even under our pillows, not just because we actively make a choice every morning to look at the news in the world or what our friends are doing. We do it because we *love* what the phone gives us. There is an ancient call in us that taps the spigot of our desires until the ritual becomes worshipful and mundane.

Now let me pause for a second just to clarify a few of these words since we will be using them throughout the book. There is some overlap and similarity between the words *habit*, *ritual*, and *routine*. They all are repeated behaviors. But a *routine* is mundane (tying your shoe). A *habit* is something that goes a lot deeper into our desires and drives and loves—a repeated action that is difficult to give up or alter (for good or bad). And *ritual* to me is a habit of *meaning*. A repeatable action that draws us into a sacred moment. Throughout this book we will mostly be talking about the last two (habits and rituals), as they are ways of becoming like Jesus that many of us have forgotten about.

Now let's talk about habits a little longer. We are a collection of our habits. And the reason habits are stickier and harder to shift or change is that they usually drive deep down into our *loves*. Our telos (our vision of the good life) is revealed through our habits. And our habits are simply the things we love deeply without ever realizing it. What we love has the power to control us and give our lives meaning and depth and richness (or it promises to, and severely underdelivers).

I am in a marriage, thankfully, where both of us understand God's design for the world, particularly the need for a cup of coffee every day, first thing in the morning. Unfortunately, I also have a spouse who thinks that even though we both enjoy coffee freshly made at 6:00 a.m., she should rarely if ever be the one to make it. If I went to bed before her, I used to assume she would prepare it before coming to bed and set the coffee timer for the morning, but then I'd wake up to find that the coffee was not made, bringing me close to passing out as I made it half-awake. (I'm only joking; if it's not made, I only tend to twitch a little in my right eye before I'm able to brew it.)

Now, coffee is not just about a cup of caffeine but is more about the dance of the morning ritual. The smell conjures up deep and fond memories of quiet, tranquil morning time, with journals and books and thinking. Drinking our morning coffee has become loaded with meaning, with immense attachment and imagery for our daily lives.

Because of the meaning of our repeated pattern, I have become the chief designated coffee maker in our family. And guess what? Alyssa genuinely thanks me for it. She's mentioned multiple times that this little act of service and blessing every single night has shown immense thoughtfulness and love to her.

I'll admit, though, that when I first began to take over

the coffee preparation, I felt very gentlemanly and chival-rous and sacrificial (in the tiniest way, obviously, because marriage is ultimately made up of one thousand micro-scopic opportunities to sacrifice for each other rather than one big sacrifice, right?). Now I essentially do it out of ritual, with a little mix of duty. But it's still an act of love. And con-tinually doing it, even once it got mundane, is maybe even more an act of love.

I think following Jesus with rhythm is the same. Even when it becomes dry for a season, it's not necessarily legal-istic, but Jesus folks often expect following Jesus to always be free and fun and spontaneous and never ritualistic or liturgical. And if it is, we cry legalism.

But what if it's right in the middle?

Take the coffee again. I set myself up for failure if I expect to serve my wife only when I feel like it, or to make the coffee only on the mornings when my love for her is really pumping in my veins that day. A lot of us do that with Jesus. I call this "following the camp high, not Jesus."

But it would also be equally bad if I made the coffee every morning purely out of duty and harbored bitterness while thinking, *Why doesn't she ever make the coffee for me?*

Making the coffee every day, even when I don't feel like it, is a way to show my love for her in faithful and non-spectacular ordinariness. I don't call that legalism. I call that holiness. Love isn't just a verb or noun. Love is a habit.

Governments have figured out this truth (the Pledge

of Allegiance, anyone?), while many churchgoers in the Protestant traditions are still calling anything repetitive "legalism." For too long we've confused legalism with something that takes effort or discipline. Just because we do something over and over doesn't mean it's legalistic.

If we cry legalism whenever we do something with repetition or effort or discipline or when something has the potential to become dry and rote, then by that definition Jesus was one of the most legalistic people we know, praying the Shema prayer at least three times a day as any faithful Jew of the first century would have been expected to do.

Legalism isn't defined by behavior. You can't look at a certain behavior and know immediately that it's legalism, because the same behavior can be done in both holy and unholy ways. While the Pharisees are typically thought of as the enemies of Jesus and are the ones we most often picture in our minds when we hear the word *legalism*, many biblical scholars believe Jesus was a Pharisee too—or at least his beliefs and expansion of Torah more closely aligned with the Pharisees than with any other group in the New Testament, including the Sadducees, the scribes, and the zealots.

But the idea isn't to do things that take repetition. It's to make sure your heart is right if you do.

I once heard someone say that rules before love equals legalism, and love before rules equals gospel formation.[9] How much power, vitality, depth, and richness have we evangelicals left on the table of church history or tradition simply because we thought it looked and smelled too "legalistic"? We can all be ritualistic whether we like to admit it or not.

We read the New Testament and think, *I can't believe people had to dress a certain way back then because of certain customs and codes.* Yet today, we might think a church is out of touch or not relevant if the worship pastor isn't wearing skinny jeans, and the pastor isn't preaching from an iPad.

Philosopher James K. A. Smith made the beautiful observation that the first and last words Jesus spoke in the gospel of John are often overlooked, even though they're very much at the heart of how we change. Jesus asked, "Do you love me?"

We are not who we are because we thought our way there. We are who we are because we loved something and chased it, often unwittingly, and we continued to do it, over and over like a liturgy. Or as Smith put it, "Love-shaping practices."[10]

All our liturgies are pointing us somewhere. The practices we do to shape and cultivate our loves are shaping us. And if that's true, liturgy isn't something you do. It's better defined as something being done to you.

We are a culture that leans heavily toward the intellectual, so we are determined to point out harmful ideas, or at least ones we disagree with. But because we don't understand that most ideas don't enter our lives through thinking them but rather practicing them unwittingly, then those ideas are able to sneak into our culture in a Navy Seal Team Six sort of way, changing us and shaping us and forming us before we even realize they're there.

And frankly the people who seem to best understand that we are creatures of love and desire, not thoughts, are the current giant tech companies of the world. Think about how Apple exists with a temple-like space (tell me their retail stores don't feel so "set apart" from the ordinary retail design that it doesn't immediately conjure up sacred feelings) where you go to sacrifice (enormously large portions of your money) to obtain that which you are looking for—connection, meaning, and depth. People stand in line all night, some even camping out on the sidewalk, for the latest device that offers those implicitly understood benefits. This phone can, and will, be more than a phone.

I think it's even fair to say that Apple is a religion with Steve Jobs as a priest (who has become a venerated secular saint after his death), mediating between man and God to give us what we want. Connection. Power. God-like knowledge of good and evil.

And we take the phone, and we crouch and bend over.

Usually with heads bowed.

Laser focused on something. Blocking out all around us.

We are silent and solemn. Tending not to speak.

And then we perform a certain behavior over and over and over again. Sound familiar?

Swipe.

Swipe.

Swipe.

Pull down.

Swipe.

Swipe.

Swipe.

Flick.

Flick.

Pull down.

You go to the Middle East and it's not uncommon to hear a bell ring throughout the day, which means it's time to pray and worship. In the West, we aren't much different. We hear that *ping* and most of us implicitly believe, *It's time to pray and worship.*

People hear the bell and get out their mats.

We hear the bell and we pull out our phones.

It seems we aren't just doing something. Screens and phones are doing something to us.

And Apple even operates on its own liturgical calendar with specific and rhythmic dates (what religion tends to call "high holy days," where we get our word *holiday* from) for new releases and launches. Steve Jobs captured the allure of the product launch. Most people won't show up if you tell them you're unveiling a new car or even your new model of Android phones. Yet Jobs, and now Tim Cook, have managed to fill theaters year after year with a religious fervor and excitement about what Apple products will be unveiled for that year. Jobs turned the fervor of "what new iPhone is coming out this year" into not just a consumer event but a religious event.

No one knew better than Steve Jobs that we are story creatures, not information creatures. We don't want facts; we want a way of life. We don't want the answers; we want a vision of what is good.

And it's no coincidence Apple became the first company in history to hit the one-trillion-dollar market cap. The greatest storytellers always win, and Apple sure has.

Even in its commercials, Apple tells stories. In one ninety-second spot, a family is at grandma and grandpa's house for the Christmas festivities. The whole family is laughing and enjoying one another, yet throughout the video one of the young teenage boys is on his phone. The commercial is set up with beautiful, emotional music to give you all the feels about how awesome Christmas is and how beautiful and amazing and family-centric it is. Yet they are purposely invoking a slight tension as you watch and wonder, *Hmmm . . . who is this boy? And why is he on his phone the whole time? He's missing all the important moments.*

And that's when the last scene cuts to the living room, with the whole extended family packed on the floor and couches, with their Christmas PJs and socks on, sipping hot cocoa facing the TV. The young teenage boy gets their attention and then turns the TV on and begins to play a little video. And the video is basically a little highlight video he put together of his family the last few days while they were together. That's why he'd had his phone out. He was making a family movie.

Everyone begins to tear up and cry and hug and thank him for the special gift to the family, then it cuts to "Happy Holidays," and the Apple logo.

The end.

There were absolutely no details or information about what the phone could do. Not how fast it is or how many megapixels it has.

Because Apple knows that's not what they're selling. They aren't trying to sell you on what the phone does. They're trying to paint a vision of the beautiful life their phone can give you.

I'll admit, the first time I watched that commercial, I thought it was touching and beautiful. But then I wondered, what is the commercial really saying? That the things I so desperately want in life—connection, meaning, deep sense of family—this phone can give me? That's a big promise. And I'm not sure anyone has checked back in to see if they've really delivered.

Once we realize that our daily habits are forming us on a fundamental level (and even more once they become micro rituals, which are the things we do every day without really realizing them), then we will start paying attention. We begin to ask, are these doing something to me I don't particularly like or want but don't realize?

With all the information we have access to, we want to optimize everything. Our cars have chips. Our phones have chips. Our Fitbits have chips. All to track and give us data we didn't even know we needed so we can make adjustments.

We audit our finances. Our diet. Everything.

What would it look like if we looked at the books of our micro liturgies?

Because here's the thing: You are becoming someone and something. You are being formed. You are an image that is *reflecting*.

But we need to resist reflecting and participating in the hustle that turns us into something we aren't.

Why?

Because I want to be more than an efficient, driven, ambitious, goal-oriented, achievement-based human. When I envision that person in the future, I don't see a loving human presence. I see a machine. That's what most of us are pointing our telos toward without realizing it.

Yet there's a bigger and better and more truthful telos that our hearts long for deep down. The telos of flourishing as the image of God found in Jesus. True humanness. That is the goal and the objective. And that is what we lost the minute that fateful curse in the garden shattered it all. But we can find our way back. How? *Through the truly human one—Jesus.*

I want to be formed and shaped and molded into *his image. To be more like him. To look like him.* To walk at his pace. To respond to the world with his gentleness and grace. To reign and rule, build, create, and cultivate under his loving and sacrificial authority. But to do that, I have to look in his face. Meet with him. Stay at his feet. Spend time with him. To live in repeatable practices and formations that consistently put myself before him. I have to shape my space and my habits away from my false self and push myself into becoming a true full image bearer of him.

2.

THIS IS WHERE IT WAS
ALWAYS HEADED

Personal and individual freedom is a cancer.

In its truest form, cancer is unchecked cell growth. It begins when something normal and good—the growth and life cycle of cells—is damaged by a tiny mutation so that the cells become monstrous and create a deformity in our bodies. Unchecked, that cell growth becomes a disease. A tumor.

I think our idea of personal and individual freedom is similar.

Why?

Freedom is amazing. And the upholding of the individual and all the rights afforded to each person in our society, sometimes at great cost, is the blessing and joy of Western society and our modern world. We are reaping immense benefits from our fight for personal freedom.

But when individual freedom becomes more than just a really helpful and good idea, when it becomes our god and our religion, when it becomes ultimate, then it is an object of worship. It turns into our vision of the good life, the thing we put first and pursue our entire lives.

At its roots, freedom was motivated by the desperate desire to escape tyranny and oppression. When the idea of classic liberalism started to sweep over the world a few hundred years ago, it had significant results. But freedom from the damage and limitations of tyranny has slowly morphed and shortened into the American gospel of freedom from limits. All limits. All hindrances. If it stands in the way of our desires and what we want, it's wrong and harmful and bad according to our culture's current view.

Today, that is our ultimate goal and telos. And where it was always leading.

Our culture beats into us the belief that our lives will be richer and better and more meaningful, and we will finally flourish, finally reach our best selves, when we remove all obstacles and limits standing in our way.

From the lightbulb to the automobile, we have invented

new ways to reduce the barriers of time, speed, and power, and in so doing, we also have simultaneously disconnected ourselves from our humanity—from family, from sleep, from our neighborhoods, from community, from craft, from time, from rest, and from who we are.

Have we considered some of the ramifications of our advancements and, ultimately, our choices? Have we counted the cost? Because we're paying for it. We've made our beds and it's time to sleep in them—yet we can't. We're drained. And buzzing. Or is that our phone? Maybe it's both—our souls and our devices, both humming with anxiety.

The world is now at our fingertips at all times. We can have just about anything we want, things our grandparents only dreamed of. We are told there's nothing we can't work hard enough for, go into enough debt for, dream enough for, set enough goals for. We only need to work harder, hustle more, sacrifice more.

But when will it be enough?

Will we ever feel more fulfilled? Will we reach a point where we are finally satisfied, when we will find *shalom*, that meaty, dense Hebrew word for peace and fullness?

The train left the station a few hundred years ago—mostly in the pursuit of good and blessing. But the tracks that were laid have had unintended consequences.

Our lopsided and monstrously disproportional elevating of personal freedom and the hustle spirit that comes with it are not taking us where we actually want to go. Our pursuit of freedom is *not actually freeing us*.

One easy place to see the harm of the hustle is in the realm of sexuality, which has seen enormous and drastic changes over a short span of fifty or so years. It was even called the sexual revolution. And revolutions scream *freedom*.

But did it make us freer?

On the surface, yes. And that was its goal.

So what does freedom mean in our culture?

Our sexual freedom means having and enjoying the most personal benefit and pleasure possible with the fewest limits, least commitment, and least sacrifice.

We have reached the logical conclusion of our views. We can see anything we could ever want or dream about sexually today. We have made the pursuit and gratification of our sexual wants and desires absolutely *frictionless*.

There is this scene in *A Beautiful Mind*, the Russell Crowe movie about the true story of Nobel-winning mathematician John Nash, where he is nudged to go chat with a girl. Because of his social awkwardness, though, he foregoes the usual dance of flirting and reading between the lines. So he goes up to a woman and instead says, "I don't exactly know what I am required to say in order for you to have intercourse with me. But could we assume that I said all that? I mean essentially, we are talking about fluid exchange right? So could we go just straight to the sex?"[1]

Now, what's most interesting about what Nash says is not that it's outrageous. Because it isn't. Rather, he is saying the actual facts without any games or hidden language.

Sex in our culture is nothing more than two consenting adults exchanging fluids as they slam their bodies together for self-gratification.

"Do you want to?" and "Are you willing?" are the only two questions that are asked for our culture's idea of sex to be fully realized. And how's that going for us?

In short, has our idea of "freedom" actually led to freedom?

Has our idea of removing all limits and restraints delivered on its promise?

It doesn't look like it. We're supposed to be more connected, yet we are easily the loneliest generation yet.

We seem to continually be creating the very opposite future to the one we want.

We are chasing freedom. Yet becoming slaves. Why?

My guess is that it's because we have a wrong and elementary view of freedom. *True* freedom has inherent restraint. Boundaries. Bumpers. And limits. But *limits* is the twenty-first-century swear word. How dare we limit someone's sexual choices, their professional aspirations, or anything else?

If we were to ask skydivers how freedom feels when they are falling out of a tiny plane about eighteen thousand feet off the ground, I'm sure the responses would be, "Exhilarating. Life changing. Exciting. Absolutely uninhibited."

Yet the reason a skydiver is able to experience true freedom in that moment is a form of restraint—the parachute. The thing meant to save is also a "limit" on the free fall.

As with skydiving, I think sexuality is most "free" in the confines and restraint of a covenantal marriage. Where there is room to discover, learn, and be free with the same person over a lifetime under a promise. Our culture tries to convince us that marriage is a prison, but it seems pretty clear that infinite sexual choice, treating sexuality how we treat food ordered on Postmates, is the opposite of free. Ultimate and unhindered choice, removing all limits, is turning us into slaves.

Our current hustle culture is no different; it's all about exceeding limits. It's about striving for that false freedom to do this. Eat that. Work this way. *Just. Work. Harder.* Network more. Just buy my masterclass and you, too, can be a millionaire by age nineteen.

I believe there is freedom in limits. Freedom in living within a design. A blueprint. An external reality. And we are trying to loosen those limits at our own peril.

What if we *can't* be anything we want to be?

What if the goal isn't to hustle but to be faithful?

What if the magic of life is found in the mundane, and it comes when we're faithful?

The Assembly Line

All it took was a bunch of dead butchered cows and pigs on moving hooks to give a CEO an idea that changed the world.

The job of an executive is usually to put out fires, lead with vision, and fix or find solutions to recurring problems, but this CEO had a particular problem he was trying to solve. He had invented something that was beginning to change and reshape the world, and he couldn't produce enough of his product fast enough. Since what he created was so innovative and different, the level of training it took to teach other men about his invention, and how to give them the skills to build this thing from scratch, was enormous. And time consuming. It took tons of focus and energy, and worse, it wasn't *scalable*—a buzzword of our tyrannical work economy today.

Then this executive remembered the meat packing industry. How one person doesn't go around to each animal and do the million steps it takes to get the cow from living animal to consumable food source on someone's plate. Instead larger-scale butcher shops had not one person doing the whole job but nineteen people standing in a line, the pigs and cows hanging on hooks, and those hooks moving down the line, while each employee stood in place and completed one small action. Over and over again. And he realized he could bring that same trick to his invention.

His name was Henry Ford.

His invention was the revolutionary Model T.

And October 7, 1913, was the first official day of the moving assembly line.

Since then, the spirit of the assembly line has turned the world upside down.

To say Ford's vision of the automobile and the assembly-line model changed the world is an understatement. It didn't just change the world. It changed how we *see* the world. How we engage the world. How we understand the world.

All of a sudden, in the span of a few years, people were able to move in ways they had only dreamed of.

Prior to Ford's invention, most people were confined to the few dozen miles around their villages and neighborhoods. That's why small towns in the rural south are only about three to four miles long; that was about the average distance people were willing to walk and the maximum length people would transport cargo by cart and horse. It was a *big* deal, and quite a "road trip," as we call it, to go to the next town over.

But now, with the automobile and the necessary roads that came right after, humans felt free. No more limits. They could go anywhere. It was the first time in history that people used some mode of transportation on a larger and more consistent basis "just because." People started to get in cars and drive anywhere—no destination in mind. They'd go for a drive just because it was fun and they felt the power of freedom. This is where we get the word *joyride*.

Leisure, happiness, freedom, and the pursuit of those things in themselves started to elevate to new levels in 1913.

Consumption was the new god.

Banker Paul Mazur of Lehman Brothers during this time knew this was a big shift banks and other powerful people could massively profit from if they intentionally pointed us in that direction. Their reasoning amounted to this: We must shift America from a needs culture to a desires culture. People must be trained to desire, to want new things even before the old has been entirely consumed. Man's desires must overshadow his needs.[2]

And here's the truth—the assembly line isn't just something we did. It was something done to us.

We are assembly-line creatures.

This invention tilted the world in a different direction and changed everything.

If hustle needed a birthdate I'd say it was the day the assembly line was born. It made efficiency a god. It made time a god. It created the ultimate pursuit of profit over everything. It gave us the operating principle of giving the least amount of energy for the highest return.

That's the premise of all the podcasts we listen to. The side hustle podcasts. The dude bro lifehack podcasts. The over-the-top passionate and yelling entrepreneur who is actually not saying much of anything–type podcasts.

Or our goal behind our side hustle and Instagram-famous businesses.

Today, even our salvation model (or our personal development model or business model) is essentially replicating that day in 1913—over and over and over again.

We've created an assembly-line Christianity. Instead of investing in relationships and one-on-one interactions with other people, we just bring our friends to church and place them on the conveyor belt of the "Sunday service," where in ninety minutes they can get a good spiritual feeling, sing some songs, hear an encouraging message, get a coffee, and then hear the pastor tell them that if they want to follow Jesus to "pray this prayer." It'd take too much time to connect each one of those people with another person in the church and maybe have a family or person "adopt" this person spiritually to walk with them, ask them hard questions, eat meals together . . . so let's just have everyone repeat after me.

Now, do I think Jesus is still active and alive and present and moving here? Of course. But I think that's despite us, not because of us.

And I'm not saying the assembly-line-built car is evil either. The car is incredible.

What I am saying is, *there are always tradeoffs.*

Concessions. Ramifications. Changes.

Have we even thought about these? Are we okay with them? Sometimes we don't even need to change anything to find a better path—just being aware of how things are shaping us is enough to affect us.

Cars allowed us to go farther and do more. But they also created a nation of consumers, creating essentially the first large-scale manufactured product that everyone wanted and was able to get.

Pesticides help us kill insects that ruin our crops. But pesticides also kill us.

The lightbulb has given us the ability to do countless things. Yet now we cheat the night and we sleep worse than any other time in history because our circadian rhythms are disrupted.

We started to value more privacy, so backyards got bigger and front porches got smaller.

All of a sudden we don't know our neighbors, and privacy is our goal.

Because of cars and technology and affluence, we don't *need* to know our neighbors. We are self-sustaining. The old stereotype of asking a neighbor for butter or sugar when in need isn't even necessary anymore. Just hit a few buttons on that rectangular glowing device in your pocket and Amazon's Prime Now program will have sugar delivered right to your door (while paying their workers a brutal and oppressive wage to get it there). Amazon is our new neighbor. And not a friendly one.

Whether we realize it or not, we treat everything we touch in life—relationships, possessions, our jobs, and more—as nothing more than the plastic straw we get every time we get a drink from the drive-through. Disposable.

Only meant to serve in the immediate. And we create a churn-and-burn culture where it's all about what I can get out of something, for the least amount of work and the most amount of benefit and convenience.

We are like the frog in the water. We don't realize the temperature has slowly been climbing since the minute that first Model T rolled off the assembly line.

Writer David Foster Wallace tells the story of "two young fish swimming along, and they happen to meet an older fish swimming the other way, who nods at them and says, 'Morning, boys, how's the water?' And the two young fish swim on for a bit, and then eventually one of them looks over at the other and goes, 'What the hell is water?'"[3]

And here's the interesting part. When something is that new (only two or three generations old) it is still very much an experiment. The jury is still out. Just because it feels like how things have always been done, we have to recognize it's the opposite. We radically altered and changed everything about how we live and organize society—from the assembly line to the industrialization of every market, including farming to clothing—and it would do us all a service to pause. There have been other ways to do life in the past, and those who resist the cultural push presently have other ways too. An experiment needs a period in which we stop, look at what is happening, and ask, *How's this going for us?*

In 1820 about 70 percent of the entire US labor force were farmers. We were a *nation* of farmers.

Today? About 1.5 percent.[4]

There are two words that describe that massive shift.

Industrial Revolution.

The time period when we fundamentally changed how we work, live, commune, and see many things in life.

Now here's the thing—I don't think we need to return to owning more farms. But I do think that jumping from an agrarian society to an industrial one so quickly has created collateral damage. We need to ask, did we lose anything when we lost that way of life?

I think so.

Though, of course, the benefits have been massive in terms of productivity. Our scale of food production has lowered food costs, and other industries have given us tons more benefits.

But what did it cost us?

The first is that agriculture and industrialization tend to approach work in fundamentally different ways.

Farmers tend to submit to limits. The limits of the weather, seasons, soil, and crops.

Proponents of industrialization do the opposite. The telos changes. It's primarily driven by the gods of profit and efficiency, so it tends to buck the limits. To look for any way to possibly cheat the system for a bigger yield that is also cheaper and better.

The spirit of innovation is a blessing and it's what made us so successful in many areas today. It's a keystone to our culture. However, we certainly have lost the visual reminders found in the soil, sun, water, and seasons that tell us we are creatures of limits.

And creatures of ritual.

Poet and author Wendell Berry says, in the same way the industrial mind (of production, mass efficiency, and disintegration) has snuck into farming (think chemicals and machines to get more out of less), the flip side and good news is that an agrarian mind can be a part of an industrial lifestyle.[5]

Meaning the train has left the station. We aren't going back to being an agrarian society. But we can bring some agrarian principles to our work and industrialized mind-set.

You might ask, *What makes something agrarian?* I believe it's rhythms. Ritual. Seasons. And integration.

Rituals are the habits of meaning that give us an anchor and add depth to our lives. The repeatable practices that come preloaded with sacred imagery and beauty. While we still have rituals in our Western lives, such as weddings and funerals, we have for the most part gotten rid of them or no longer believe in them. Yet most minority communities have wisely held on to this richness and depth of ritual. Think of how a Hispanic girl is given a quinceañera at age fifteen, or think of a Jewish bar mitzvah. It's an enormously rich and beautiful celebration, marking the transition from childhood to an adulthood of meaning and responsibility.

In contrast, our predominant cultural ethos with rites

or rituals of passage is much cheaper. Much flimsier and less meaningful. We mark no serious transition in the teenage years and call them to nothing of importance or serious leadership or responsibility at that age, so instead by default their moment of transition becomes when we give them an iPhone and a driver's license. Essentially saying, *Instead of connecting you to the community, we're giving you a device that connects you to other people who know and love you less, not us. And a piece of plastic with your picture on it that can take you toward other people and away from us.*

Rhythm is living life with music and cadence. It's coming back to something big or small, again and again, as a way of remembering and reminding. Think of rhythms as your daily vitamins of nourishment, which is different from an ordinary routine. Routine is oatmeal, while rhythms are the fancy dinner at a Michelin three-star restaurant. They both feed you and offer you life, but one is a high experience, and the other is a forgettable but necessary one. My having to mow the lawn once a week is a routine. Our family having a big blowout Shabbat dinner together every Friday night is a rhythm. It is the high moment of our week, a practice we have cultivated over the past five years of setting one full day apart for our family for resting, delighting in Jesus, filling up our tanks, and dancing to the music of grace. You know the high point of Thanksgiving, with the feast and party atmosphere and all your family and friends gathered together around a table?

That's what we try to do in miniature every single Friday night. That is our rhythm.

As a culture, we're losing ritual and we are losing rhythm. We're losing rootedness and depth and anchoredness. Because time and rhythm and ritual, these things are no longer external forces that we must submit to. They're things we can bend, hack, destroy. Or so we think.

And how's that going for us?

A Better Ritual

One of the peculiar parts of a secular society like ours is, no matter how hard we run away from something that is sacred and wired into our DNA, we still end up with it in various forms.

For example, we have lost many of our rituals or rites of passage. Well, with the exception of a few places—namely in gangs.

We wonder why people flock to rites like this, but we are creatures of meaning—we are hunting for it and pursuing it our whole lives, whether we realize it or not. Our entire life has us metaphorically nose to the ground trying to catch the faintest scent of something that will make us feel something. We are desperate for depth and wholeness and fulfillment. Craving and crawling for every sense of meaning and richness we can find.

Another way to put it is, we can't live without *purpose*.

And something about that purpose gives us an anchoring that nothing else can. Even amid horrible circumstances.

It's why Viktor Frankl said, in *Man's Search for Meaning*, his famous book that chronicles his time in a Nazi concentration camp, the people who were most likely to survive the brutality of the concentration camp were those who held on to a purpose. They had *meaning*.[6]

We can't live without it.

One woman in Auschwitz refused to let the concentration camp and its brutal conditions prevent her from honoring Shabbat, a ritual of meaning and purpose, so every Friday she would save the tiny bit of margarine she received and use it to make two little candles, even taking some threads from her dresses to make the wicks. And every Friday night, in the midst of one of the worst displays of evil of our recent times, she resisted. They could take her freedom. Take her resources. Take everything, including her life. But they couldn't take away the meaning of her Friday ritual of lighting candles before sunset to usher in the Jewish Sabbath and welcome God into her soul no matter where she stood—even in a concentration camp.

Those little candles were an act of resistance.[7] An act of defiance. They connected her to God and to the people who shared that same faith. They gave her the strength of community. They were her way of saying, *You might be able to take away my home, my possessions, and my relationships,*

*but you can't take away my meaning. My identity. My core
sense of purpose.*

So the question quickly becomes, how can we uproot our
cheaper rituals and replace them with something much better? Most of our ritualistic behaviors are oriented toward
gratifying our five senses, such as making coffee right on the
dot at 6:00 a.m. because we can't live without the caffeine. Or
for so many of us, grabbing our phone off the nightstand the
minute we wake up so we can participate in the ritual of the
tap and scroll. These aren't connected to a deeper meaning;
they're just oriented toward consumption and self.

Searching for likes and comments on social media
might actually be the biggest ritual of our time—a full-
blown religion with the sacrifice being ourselves, the priest
being Mark Zuckerberg, and the god we are worshiping
being the god of *someone tell me I'm good enough.* We want
to be accepted, and we feel we can do that if we receive
daily micro-affirmations from people we barely know, or
have the latest information or gossip about our friends and
the popular celebrities on YouTube or other social media.

That's why I always find it a little funny when news
articles bemoan the death of religion: "Millennials are leaving the church!"

No they aren't. They are just going to a different one.

We are faithful churchgoers—to the church of *self.* Or

swiping right every weekend. Or the temple of Coachella and Burning Man, where we rapturously worship our cultural gods and icons named Beyoncé and Kendrick Lamar.

Things we come back to, again and again, in search of meaning.

It's interesting how we scoff at ancient cultures, with brutal and barbaric rites of passage, like the Mawé people who subject their boys to stings from bullet ants, one of the most painful insect stings in the world. (On the Schmidt's pain index of one to four, the bullet ant is rated a four plus.) A glove made from leaves is filled with the ants, and the boys must wear it for twenty minutes while dancing amid the community as a rite of initiation from boyhood to manhood. Barbaric? Perhaps. But what if they are on to something? What if having some transition practice is better than what we don't have (minus the parts that make us cringe)? The methods might be suspect, but I can imagine the lesson of "I'm no longer a child meant to primarily receive but now a leader in this community primarily structured to brunt and absorb pain on behalf of those I'm now serving and leading" is a worthy lesson many of us would've been better off to receive.

Do you think it's just a coincidence that we have a crisis of extended adolescence, with boys having no vision and purpose and many still wasting their thirties doing things that were inappropriate even in their teens, like sleeping around, playing video games, taking no responsibility for their lives, and leeching off of family and friends?[8] We wander, trying to "find ourselves." Yet self-discovery in our culture is just another way to self-destruction.

A recent writer for *National Geographic* spent some time with the Bukusu tribe in western Kenya and witnessed their boys' painful transition to manhood around age fourteen. It ends in their circumcision, standing up, surrounded by their tribe. The writer, rightly horrified, also left with a feeling of uneasiness.

"Dismay aside, I found it hard not to grudgingly admire a culture that gives boys such an unambiguous path to manhood. The steps are clearly marked. The knife and the cut undeniably make the whole business real."[9]

Unfortunately, it's very much in the spirit of the West to think that we are not only more advanced than tribal cultures but also more than glad to have left behind all their uncivilized practices. And while there surely have been advances in how we structure culture, I wonder what we've lost. Have we left behind some of the things we believed were harmful but replaced them with an anxiety-ridden, insanely overconnected, self-absorbed, individualistic society?

I'll tell you what we have left behind.

We left behind meaning. And I want it back.

Burning Out

"Jeff, Alyssa is the smoke alarm of your family. You'd do well to listen to her before your life burns down."

Those words came from our mentors. Alyssa and I had reached the marital impasse I mentioned earlier. We were going in circles, having the same arguments in the same way, over and over. We knew we needed help, so we called them and laid it all out.

I can't remember many times someone's brief comments changed my life. But that was one of those moments.

This was about five years ago. I was headed for burnout, and I was bringing my family with me. We had just moved to Hawaii, and I was doing a million things for work, all with not much direction or purpose. I was flying all around the country for speaking engagements probably thirty or so weekends a year, while my wife was at home with an almost two-year-old, and a baby in her belly.

I don't think most people realize this, but Hawaii is literally farther away from any other place in the world. That is, there is more ocean between Hawaii and the next sizeable urban land mass than anywhere else in the world. So to say I had to travel around the world for four days just to speak somewhere for thirty minutes was completely accurate.

I'd speak, hop back on a plane, and fly for two days straight, get home exhausted, look at my wife who was sinking, and try to pretend like I never left. (Which does not work at all, by the way. We've come to learn when I travel on rare occasions now that there's a two- to three-day readjustment period for everyone.)

But here's the hard part—I really enjoyed it and wanted to travel and speak. It was fun. And it was fulfilling! I come alive when I get to chat with other people about big ideas.

But it wasn't sustainable. And it wasn't the best for me or our family. It was leading to chaos.

I never actually paused to ask: Does this fit into our family's rhythm?

Is there a way to live so I don't lose my humanness, but actually live in it? Where instead of hustling I would concentrate on becoming?

The world's idea of success might be to do a bunch of stuff—write a book, start a business, go hike that mountain, say no to more kids. But is it success? I mean, of course we are supposed to work hard. Work well. And say yes to good things that come our way. But is there a line? Is it ever enough?

What if God's idea of success isn't about what you do, but who you are? What if the goal of following Jesus is actually about becoming fully human? Stepping into the person you were created to be and resisting our culture's worship of speed, hustle, activity, noise, fame, and knowledge?

We need to resist the noise and speed of the air and, instead, embrace the slowness of Jesus.

We need to value what our culture doesn't.

It's time to stop doing and start becoming.

MUSIC FROM CHAOS

Orison Marden was a writer in the late 1800s. For one particular writing project, he set out to discover and interview a giant of his day and ask the secret behind his impact on the world. One of Marden's first questions was about this remarkable man's "untiring energy and phenomenal endurance."[1]

The response? This man had worked an average of twenty hours per day for the past fifteen years. This meant he had not just been awake for twenty hours straight, which in itself would've been brutal, but he had averaged twenty hours a day *working. For fifteen years.*

In fact, he worked so much that he would joke that even though he was forty-seven years old at the time of those comments, he was more like eighty-two years old, since if you calculated how many eight-hour workdays he fit into his twenty-hour workdays it would have made him about that age.[2]

It's not a coincidence that this person thought work and productivity were so important that he made it one of his missions to kill the thing that most stood in his way—sleep. He hated sleep. He even called it a "heritage from our cave days."[3] It was as if he just couldn't believe society hadn't progressed past this wasteful activity.

Who was this person? This man who hated sleep and was an obscene workaholic almost certainly to the extreme detriment of his health?

Well, the very person who made it his mission to create and invent things that would allow him to cheat the very thing he hated.

Thomas Edison.

The year?

It was 1879, the year our culture made a tradeoff we haven't fully reckoned with—the lightbulb.

Something Edison firmly believed could take us out of the "cave days," even going so far to remark how he believed artificial light seemed to make people more intelligent:

> When I went through Switzerland in a motor-car, so
> that I could visit little towns and villages, I noted the

effect of artificial light on the inhabitants. Where water power and electric light had been developed, everyone seemed normally intelligent. Where these appliances did not exist, and the natives went to bed with the chickens, staying there until daylight, they were far less intelligent.[4]

Ah, yes, that's it. When your lightbulb is on, you must be a smarter person. I wonder if that's where we got the funny cultural symbol of a lightbulb over someone's head when they have a big idea.

In fact, it is. Many photographs were taken of Edison holding a lightbulb, and over time, instead of saying someone was smart or inventive, we started saying they were "bright."

It's a funny thing how belief gets born into the world.

We create what we want to see. We are motivated by our vision for the world.

Edison hated sleep, so he invented something that helped him cheat it—and it forever altered how we structure life. Before Edison, when the sun set, your main activity concluded for the day. After Edison, that was the moment it was starting.

Now, not only does today's research completely contradict Edison's view on sleep, but it's no coincidence that the invention he is most famous for is actually the single most responsible device for sleep disruption and quality for the past 130 years. We have used it to cheat ourselves out of the rest we need as we hustle and push against limits.

It's clear that we need to sleep. We start short-circuiting and breaking down if we don't. When we don't get adequate sleep, we increase our dementia risk by 33 percent, and the risk is much higher for depression and anxiety and loss of memory. We literally lose years off our lives—they say chronic sleep deprivation carves three to five years off the ages of our brains. We're almost 50 percent more likely to develop heart disease, three times more likely to catch a cold, 50 percent more likely to be obese, and our body starts having crazy hormonal imbalances, which affects our cravings, appetites, and more.[5]

We want to squeeze more and more out of less and less, so we continue to cheat in other ways too, including with the soil that grows our food.

Our fertilizing techniques have actually changed the composition of soil as we once knew it, leading to the law of diminishing returns. Most farmland is no longer allowed to recover, and the nutrients that reset it are gone. So, what's our solution for "fixing" the problem? We use more fertilizer.

Our modus operandi is to push the limits as far as they can go, and when we hit a wall, we find some chemical or drug to step in and help us artificially push further. Both the soil and our bodies get exhausted—literally, we deplete the life from them. The answer to this is crop rotation, where we steadily rotate certain patches of agriculture in a cadence of work and rest. Yet economically that is difficult for farmers, so some decide to squeeze out a few more dollars in the short term by using all the fields all the time. Sounds a lot like our bodies, right? Made for a balance of work and rest but powered by the god of economics, we would rather push the limits to extract some cash.[6]

A cycle of cheating the darkness and the fields and our bodies. Because we want to get there faster.

A cycle of extortion. Because we want more out of something than they're willing or able to give.

And of playing God. Because God doesn't have limits, and humans do. And we'd much rather be the former.

But what if in trying to be God, we've forgotten how to be human?

To actually live *within* our limits. To believe there's rhythm in things that can make us more whole again. To believe things like silence are a gift. That sabbath is a gift. And that obscurity, the place of being unknown and not famous, which is the telos for most of us, isn't a curse but an enormous gift.

We are scrambling. We are tired. We are burned out.

We are creatures of chaos, by nature of the curse, where sin flooded into God's holy and good creation and is de-creating and unraveling all that is good and holy. And we are still de-creating ourselves and our world today.

Yet we know we were born as creatures of meaning, by nature of the creation account.

We feel it in our bones. We see it in our lives. It plays out in our minds, marriages, jobs, and hearts.

It's why we somehow can work sixty hours a week at our job, but when our spouse asks for a date night an hour every Monday, we say we don't have time. Or that it's "too much."

It's why we press a bunch of buttons on a computer for work all week and somehow get to Friday and wonder, *What even did I do all week? What did I accomplish?*

It's why we feel like there is this external force in the world just dragging us through our days and our responsibilities and priorities, and we feel taken prisoner by the god of urgency and hurrying and chaos.

But you know what's funny?

Chaos isn't new.

It was here first.

In the Beginning

"The earth was waste and void, darkness covered the abyss, and a mighty wind was blowing over the surface of the waters" (Gen. 1:1–2, paraphrase).

In the beginning . . . The earth was *tohu wa-bohu* (Hebrew). Guess what *tohu* can be translated as?

Chaos.

The earth was chaos and desolation. Darkness covered the abyss, and the Spirit of God was hovering over the waters.

It's no secret in ancient Jewish culture that water

represented primordial forces of evil and darkness and chaos. So the stage set in the first page of Scripture is that of chaos and darkness.

And yet we find the Spirit there.

Hovering.

The only other place we find the word translated as "hovering" in the Scriptures is in Deuteronomy 32:11 where it describes a mother bird flapping and beating her wings over her babies. Covering them and encouraging them to fly.

God isn't scared of chaos in our lives.

He won't disappear. He's not distant.

But he does encourage us to fly.

And so what's the antidote to chaos? To the splintering and fracturing of all things?

It's *shalom,* which means "peace." But when we say the word *peace* in English, some of us think of the seventies psychedelic hippie peace, and that's not what *shalom* means. In fact, every letter in Hebrew that makes up the word *peace* is trying to tell us something.

Shalom in Hebrew is שלם.

But let's break down those three letters because, in Hebrew, each letter can have its own meaning (and also keep in mind Hebrew is read from right to left).

מ Mem: water, chaos

ל Lamed: the staff, authority

ש Shin: teeth, destroy, consume

True shalom carries weight. It means to have the teeth to destroy the authority of chaos.

And even better, guess what *Jerusalem* means?

It's a combination of two words—*yeru* and *shalom*. And *yeru* can be translated as "you will see."

So Jerusalem means "you will see the mouth of peace destroy the authority of chaos." It's the city where peace and blessing and fullness reigns.

Where darkness is cast out.

Light is shining.

And in some ways I think Jerusalem is a metaphor or destination for us all.

It's not a coincidence that at the very end of the Scriptures, the place God designed to be the finish line of our story—where all things are made new—is called the "new Jerusalem" (Rev. 21:2).

All of us are pilgrims on this journey. We're either walking toward chaos or putting one foot in front of the other on our long and arduous journey toward the city of peace and shalom. The new Jerusalem.

The End of Chaos

I remember the fiery, visceral hurt like it was yesterday. But it wasn't yesterday. It was a decade ago.

And I was in *pain*.

Not from a physical accident, but from my life choices. My first serious girlfriend had broken up with me—the one I thought I'd marry. And since I didn't know what I wanted to do with my life except marry her, I felt lost. Without direction. Like I was pushed into a coffin and buried underground alive. Chest beating but with no room to go anywhere.

That's when I had the first thought of ending it. Only people who have been there understand, but there is a point at which emotional and mental pain can reach such extreme levels that it enters into your physical body so you feel physically sick. It feels like acid in your soul. It burns. Deeply.

So you just want it to end.

I remember sleeping. A lot. Wanting to do nothing but sleep during the day. Skipping classes. Missing important meetings or deadlines. Because the only time relief came was when my eyes were closed.

That's the only time the chaos stopped.

Those primordial waters that were rushing and tossing and churning about in the very first few sentences of Genesis seemed to be in my heart.

Just twelve months earlier, I'd had a profound encounter with Jesus in my dorm room in my little beachside university in San Diego, but I didn't feel like much was changing.

That elevated the chaotic feeling. I wondered, *Did I do this wrong? Did I miss a step?*

I'd thought that when I started to follow Jesus, things

were supposed to get better. If that was true, why was it getting worse? Why did it hurt more instead of less?

Maybe it's because when we're dead, we can't feel anything. But once we're alive, that means our senses are too.

Can a dead person feel chaos? If a corpse is caught up in a tornado, is that body really affected? It's only when we're alive that we can actually get scared when we see what's brewing.

Or maybe it's because I now was tasked with the job of turning around a freight train that had been carrying momentum for almost two decades of self-centered decisions about what I wanted. What felt best. What was best for me.

I'd thought that following Jesus would make things easier. I thought my problems would disappear.

I'm the type of person who, when I go toward something or make a change, I go all in. And that meant I was reading three books a week on theology, going to two prayer groups and Sunday services each, and participating in nineteen accountability groups (okay, that last one is an exaggeration).

But it wasn't long before I thought, *Is this* it? *I thought there was more.*

It took me years to realize all I'd done was change the clothes on my problems. They were still the same problems. I was still as disintegrated as ever. My life was still as disconnected as ever. I never actually let what I believed enter into my normal daily habits or rituals, which is where change, growth, joy, and meaning actually happen.

I was trying to build my beliefs and good morals on a foundation of chaos. I started to do a bunch of Christian things, but I was not addressing the underlying anchoring every human needs to flourish.

Here's another way to put it: the big difference between chaos and shalom is *rhythm*.

Chaos is unpredictable and unrhythmic. It has no set cadence.

But shalom is more like a dance that depends on the rhythm in music.

Have you ever stopped and wondered what makes music, *music*?

If I take a spoon and hit my bowl with it, that's not music. But if I hit my bowl with it once, then hit it again, and then again in timed increments, then that's music.

The most fundamental building block to music is rhythm. And rhythm is a funny thing if you think about it. It's the force that keeps the music going forward, but it's also something the music keeps coming back to.

Rhythm is everything.

Have you ever heard someone learn to play a new instrument? Usually they produce a collection of random notes that sound terrible. The noise is grating. It hurts your ears. There are sounds, but there's no rhythm. So, the first step is creating a tempo. Learning timing.

It reminds me of those students at high school dances whose moves made me think, *What on earth are you doing right now?* The irony is that dancing is self-expression. You can do whatever you want. There's freedom in dancing—*to a point.* Because you still have to submit to the rhythm or your moves look weird, haphazard, and cringeworthy. You have to feel the beat and find yourself in the cadence.

What if our lives are like that? What if we are dancing through life believing we're moving to a smooth rhythm, when we're actually out of sync with the beat, missing steps and bumbling along with no recognizable form? We're telling everyone how free we are, but no sane person would look at our dancing and call it *beautiful.* It looks and feels off, and we all know it when we do it ourselves. We're not following the rhythm of the music around us. So how do we find that rhythm? How do we form our dance around the steady, purposeful tempo that's in the music?

The Song in the Other Room

One of the more magical experiences Alyssa and I have ever had was going to an Adele concert. A friend surprised us with tickets, and that gift allowed us to experience Adele performing live and without a lot of production or background music. She stood in front of a crowd of twenty thousand people and sang for two hours in what was one of the most beautiful displays of human power and creativity we have ever seen.

I remember tearing up a few times—not at the emotion in the words, but at the sheer power and beauty inherent in the sound. It's not science; you can't measure it, but when you hear it, you just *know.*

Her voice was compelling. Alluring.

At one point I ran out to the car, and on the way back, I could hear her singing in the lobby and corridor of the stadium. It was that familiar yet fuzzy and muffled sound from far away. And it drew me in. There's something about good music that makes you want to go to it. Seek it out. As with a beacon or lighthouse on a cliff, you head toward the beauty.

I think God gave each of us a desire for rhythm in the music he creates. We hear a song in the other room. We hear the hum of meaning as it calls us. We try to ignore it, but we can't.

The best response is to go hunting for it. Chase it.

And when it starts getting louder, we know we're getting closer to where God is playing a symphony of shalom. It's our job to *listen and follow.* And the cool part about our walk with Jesus is, the closer we actually get to him, the clearer the music becomes. And the clearer it becomes, the better you can dance to it. I'm reminded of Aslan's music in C. S. Lewis's book *The Magician's Nephew*:

In the darkness something was happening at last. A voice had begun to sing . . . it seemed to come from all directions at once . . . Its lower notes were deep enough to be the voice of the earth herself. There were no words. There was hardly even a tune. But it was beyond comparison, the most beautiful noise he had ever heard. It was so beautiful Digory could hardly bear it.[7]

Have you ever heard music so beautiful you could hardly bear to listen to it?

That's the music God is playing. And he's inviting us to dance to it. But here's the thing we have to acknowledge about dancing before we can keep moving forward on this journey together: learning to dance takes work.

Learning to dance may feel clumsy at first. Practice is necessary if you're going to be able to dance well. You may step on someone else's toes. You may even step on your own toes.

You'll be counting the steps; that's expected. And that's what leaning into new practices will feel like. The rest of this book is me telling my story of learning those steps. New formations. New ways to live. New steps to life. To genuine humanness. To flourishing. And we have to be honest with ourselves—learning to dance is hard. It takes practice. A lot of it. It takes dedication to show up at the same time and same place every week. To do it just one more time.

Knowing that you learn to dance simply by practicing. But you'll get to a place where you stop looking down at your feet and start looking up into the eyes of Jesus as you walk through life with him in a graceful rhythm.

4.

WHY SILENCE IS SO LOUD

I'm currently writing this book at a coffee shop. And because I'm acutely aware of noise as I write about it, I just closed my eyes for a few seconds. I am trying to concentrate on all the noise around me. I can hear some indie music playing overhead, a barista sliding back the ice box lid then scooping and rattling the ice, another barista yelling "turkey bacon sandwich!" I hear cups and lids snapping together, a door opening, muffled voices at the next table, and the drive-through window opening.

It's amazing how noisy it really is for a "quiet place" that many people use for work—and how good we have gotten at being numb to the noise.

For an added dose of irony, there is a poster on the wall that says in big, bold font, "Take the sound of Starbucks with you." It's an advertisement to download the Spotify playlist they are playing when you leave.

Nah, I'm good. I don't want to take the sound with me.

Here's the reality, though: we actually *do* take noise with us. Noise is an airborne pathogen we are breathing in constantly. It gets buried in our body for better or worse. We are creatures of this earth with five senses, and hearing is one of them.

We read a lot about how our current way of doing things is harming the earth—through our machines, factories, oil spills in our oceans, waste, depletion of resources, pollution, and many other things.

But there is one I rarely hear about from politicians or those on the nightly news: *noise pollution.*

Because of the insane levels of noise in our culture, a part of the human brain is being taxed far more than in previous generations. A part of your brain that is actually meant to fight and filter the noise by "sensory gating." That's sometimes explained as the "cocktail party effect." For example, when there are a hundred people talking all in close quarters, if you have normal hearing, you have no problem being able to focus on the conversation right in front of you. Your brain is "sensory gating," or blocking out all the irrelevant noise and stimuli. You aren't actively doing it; it's just happening. Which is why when I was in Starbucks in the beginning of this chapter, I didn't hear anything at first, or it felt quiet and peaceful—until I purposely concentrated on the noises my brain was subconsciously blocking out.

This part of the brain helps us focus and not be overwhelmed by outside stimuli, from sight to touch to smell. But an increased level of noise taxes the body and brain more than it can handle. Our brains have always used the process of sensory gating. But if the sensory-gating part were a wheelbarrow, then a hundred years ago it had to carry one-pound loads. Today, though, it has to carry hundred-pound loads. That part of the brain sounds like a Ferrari engine pushing the gas pedal as hard as it can go—with no breaks. Ever.

It's affecting us in deep ways. One study in Japan found a deep connection between sensory-gating deficiency and chronic fatigue syndrome.[1] In other words, our brains are literally exhausted because of the noise. In addition, a clinical test can be given to determine your level of sensory-gating deficiency. And guess what condition is usually present in people with extremely high sensory-gating deficiency rates? Schizophrenia.[2]

I think this is interesting because we tend to think mental health is contained within an individual, whereas our culture's unprecedented noise and stimulation may also be at fault by overwhelming and exacerbating people mentally. And I think that's true even for those without a significant mental disorder.

While I'm obviously not a medical or mental health professional who can determine if noise is making us crazy, I *do* know what it's doing to me. I want to escape it, but at the same time, like an addict, I want to be back in it.

Silence is quiet. But it also roars.

Noise distracts. Numbs.

And while the white noise all around us is certainly not ideal, I don't think we realize how quickly "normal" noise crosses into damaging noise.

For instance, in a *New York Times* article from a few years ago, a reporter was curious about measurable noise levels, so he went around and measured them in the city at various spots. Granted, New York is easily one of the noisiest cities in the world, but the places he visited weren't unique to New York and are similar no matter where you are. Places like these could be found in any populated area.

One employee at a place the journalist visited said, "I've been getting migraines." So much that she would wake up with her ears ringing and buzzing, and she began taking medicine usually prescribed for seizures.

Where did this employee work? The JFK tarmac? A construction site? Nope.

She was a waitress at a restaurant. A place we go to eat and, hopefully, have deep, meaningful conversations. But during the waitress's conversations, the journalist noted, the waitress had to lean in close to hear and yell to even be heard.

And when measured, the restaurant averaged noise levels around ninety-six decibels. A level the government says is not suggested for working conditions, past the maximum of a few hours without ear protection—let alone an entire work shift, multiple times per week.[3] (And leisure conditions like eating at a restaurant should be at a lower level, yes?)

That article made me think twice about how much we have *normalized* insane levels of noise.

In fact, this has created a disagreement between Alyssa and me on almost every date night. She wants to go somewhere we can talk. I do, too, but I also want to go somewhere *exciting*, which usually means somewhere *loud*.

She rightly hates places like that because they don't allow for intimacy and connection. And I wonder why I willingly love and subject myself to places that are essentially assaulting us with the weapon of noise.

But when that *New York Times* journalist spoke with hearing-loss prevention experts, who know more about our ears than anyone else, they said people should not be exposed to any noise over one hundred decibels for more than ten to fifteen minutes. "We definitely consider those levels able to cause damage and likely to cause permanent damage with repeated exposure," said Laura Kauth, an audiologist and president of the National Hearing Conservation.[4]

Those noise levels aren't just happening on a tarmac next to an airplane jet or beneath some giant machine in a factory. They're also measured consistently in that spin class we go to in the morning and that bar we head to on Friday night.

You might be thinking, *Well, of course it's noisier these days, but it's just part of our culture. No one is doing it on purpose.* Actually, some restaurants *are.* They're weaponizing noise for profit—to speed up their table turns. Some research shows that people drink more when music is loud (read: spend more money) and chew faster (finish their meals and leave faster) when louder music is present. The noise sets your pace whether you realize it or not.

When I worked as a server in high school, it was clear that the main way to make more money was to get people to eat as fast as possible and leave as fast as possible so a new customer could sit down. In fact, the Hard Rock Cafe was built upon this premise and "had the practice down to a science, ever since its founders realized that by playing loud, fast music, patrons talked less, consumed more and left quickly."[5]

But consider a declassified CIA document detailing torture techniques at black sites during the War on Terror. It mentions "loud music" seventeen times and says that torture, specifically in Guantanamo Bay, involved heavy strobe lights and loud music.[6]

So if loud music and overstimulation and strobe lights

are used as tactics of war and torture, why do we willingly subject ourselves to them in everyday life?

Torture technique on terrorists or a rave at a club for millennials?

The same thing apparently.

What Silence Sounds Like

When I normally go to bed at night, the house is "silent." No one is speaking. No phones or tablets are on. There is no obvious noise. But one night, the power went out and it was different. It was *creepy silent.* The noise dropped from silent to terrifying. The dozens of devices that are usually receiving electricity in our house—the fridge, the modem, the vacuum charging, ceiling fans—were no longer buzzing. That was true silence. And I realized I probably hadn't heard it for ages.

What do we hear when there's no human noise at all?

George Prochnik, the author of *In Pursuit of Silence*, set out to do exactly that. Find silence. And not just any type of silence, but his goal was to find what he deemed as the quietest place in the world. This led him to Iowa and the basement of Trappist New Melleray Abbey, which is noted to be one of the quietest places on earth.

As the monk showed him the way to the basement, he warned, "the silence of the room was so intense" it was likely to take him "outside of [his] comfort zone." Some people from big cities, the monk added, find themselves "physically unable to remain in the chapel for even five minutes."[7]

When we first think of silence and solitude, we may not care much about it, or we may even think it sounds religiously sexy and hipster, cool, and trendy.

Until we try it.

And then we are shocked and maybe terrified by it.

Because in silence we feel exposed and naked, and weirdly we become noisy. Not outwardly but inside our heads. So we quickly dismiss it. *Nah, I'm good.*

But here's the unsexy and unpolished truth: our aversion to that nakedness and the awkwardness and ugliness we feel are actually why we *need* to do it. If we never experience it, we are continually buzzing, always anxious, wired, and on edge, empty and spiritually thin and malnourished.

Henri Nouwen, one of my favorite spiritual thinkers, said about his experience with silence and solitude: "Solitude is not a private therapeutic place. Rather, it is the place of conversion, the place where the old self dies and the new self is born."[8]

It's not a therapeutic place.

It's where you go to die.

He went on to say that silence is such a force because it is truly one of the only places we are laid bare. Completely naked.

No calls to make. No meetings to attend. No tasks to accomplish. No music to listen to.

It's complete nothingness. "A nothingness so dreadful that everything in me wants to run to my friends, my work, and my distractions so that I can forget my nothingness and make myself believe that I am worth something."[9]

And here's the worst part: that's just the beginning. If we stay in it longer and push through it, up bubbles a myriad of distractions, random ideas, images, and thoughts that feel so uncomfortable we wonder, *Do I really have these thoughts? Where is this coming from?*

But to stay put in the quiet place is to stay put in the desert. A place we can't survive on our own, where mirages of our false self pop up again and again. And we are desperate for someone to save us and meet us there. Thirsty for just a drop of water.

And that's where these words of Henri Nouwen speak to me over and over again as a beautiful reminder.

"The wisdom of the desert is that the confrontation with our own frightening nothingness forces us to surrender ourselves totally and unconditionally to the Lord Jesus Christ."[10]

Silence and solitude are like a graveyard for all the worst in you and your false self.

And if we want to live into our true selves, the ones Jesus created us to be, we have to enter through the graveyard. We have to take ourselves to the desert.

For more than two decades, I tried to resist this open grace. To escape silence. I was the kid who couldn't fall asleep without the TV on and who got in trouble frequently for never being quiet in class. When you think of a hyperactive, ADHD, bouncy kid, you are thinking of me.

When I started following Jesus in college, it was visceral and emotional and new and fresh and exciting. But at the same time, every time I'd get quiet and sit at his feet, it was brutal. The minute I'd get still was the minute I'd start to be tormented by vivid pictures of choices I'd made that I was wearing in my body. I felt my sin. It hurt. Some of the memories were from years before, yet in those moments I could feel them as if they'd happened five minutes ago.

I remember one angst-filled moment in particular. I'd been wanting and needing to spend time with Jesus, yet I was disillusioned with the fact that the quieter I got, the more it felt like torture. I threw my Bible across the room and yelled, "This doesn't even work!"

Silence and solitude hurt.

I began to hate it and avoid it, because I didn't like what happened or what I saw in that silence. This began a journey of doing all the Christian things I was supposed to do—praying and reading my Bible—but without ever slowing down or quieting myself.

Why didn't anyone tell me? Where did I get this picture that time alone with Jesus was therapeutic, beautiful, serene, and peaceful?

Was I doing something wrong? Was something broken?

I realized that yes—something was broken.

Me.

I married Alyssa in 2012, and anyone who is married knows that "up-closeness" can be startling. You are now joined as one, sleeping in the same bed, doing life together, and partnering on everything and anything.

When I was close with Alyssa, I started to get that sense she had something I didn't. What was it?

There was an anchoring about her. She seemed so grounded, so at ease in the slowness and the quiet and the stillness. She even seemed to pursue it! If we were busy or if our schedule was crammed that week, she'd fight to get away. Crave those moments.

Not unlike Jesus in Luke: "Jesus often withdrew to lonely places and prayed" (Luke 5:16).

Jesus voluntarily withdrew to the lonely places. On purpose.

Alyssa had that same rhythm about her, while I was afraid of the lonely places and ran as far as I could from them.

But love did what it always does. Slow and steady hits with the chisel on the rock of a heart. One hit doesn't do much. But one hit gets you to a hundred. And a hundred gets you to a thousand. And a thousand well-placed hits of the chisel create something beautiful.

And man, it was hard—and still is at times.

It took three or four years of my seeing Alyssa be comfortable with silence and actually crave it, until I began to think, *You know, I think I can try that again now.*

Maybe the very thing I was running from was actually the thing I needed most. And the pain of it was a smoke signal telling me that this was where I needed to be.

Realizing my aversion to silence and solitude is normal was the hard but necessary first step.

I knew I had two options:

I could go *around* my true self within the noise.

Or I could go *through* my true self with silence.

The beautiful part is that even though it's messy and painful and glaring, we aren't alone.

Jesus meets us there. He was waiting for us. In silence. In our pain. And let's be honest; sometimes it feels like he doesn't. But when we keep showing up—again and again—he doesn't leave us out in the cold.

As the prophet Isaiah said, Jesus gives us "streams in the wasteland" (43:19). He meets us in the place of death with sustaining life. He won't take us out of that place, but he will sustain us in it.

In fact, when we see his face in those moments, it's almost as if we're not waiting for him; it's as if he's been waiting for us. In that mundane, everyday ordinariness, we see him. Face to face. Eye to eye. And we start to hear something different.

Not noise, but his voice. *This is your true self. The one I saw when I died for you. I've been here the whole time, waiting for you to get here.*

A Quiet Revolution

When we think of famous rebels or revolutionaries or resist-
ers from history, we tend to think about noise and violence,
about warfare and a small band of militia fighters trying to
take down an empire.

Not me. I think about Fred Rogers.

Yes, Mister Rogers.

Of course, there's the urban legend he was a Navy SEAL
and wore those awesome cardigan sweaters to cover up full-
length arm sleeve tattoos. But I don't mean in that regard.

Mister Rogers was a rebel and revolutionary because of
how different he was on television. I remember watching
him as a kid and gravitating toward his peace and calm and
secure quietness—maybe because I always had such a tough
time with those exact things.

Looking back now, it's astounding to think about what
he did. How he predicated his show on calm, slow, methodical, and pointed talking. Yet silence and slowness are now
treated like diseases to be eradicated. Television inherently
calls for more noise and stimulation. The cuts and pace and
music are intentionally nothing like real life. (If only punch-
ing someone would result in a *POW!* like the old Batman
days.) In fact, especially during Mister Rogers's era, I remember cartoons growing in noise, speed, and stimulation. Today
most animated shows are an assault on the senses, causing

violence to our more sensitive awareness. Attempting to entertain and stimulate via a metaphorical electric shock that ends up frying the more fragile parts of us.

Rogers knew that, and he knew it was creating a culture of buzz and anxiety. So he fought for the opposite.

Think of the boardroom fight that must have happened at least once or twice. *Fred, you can't be silent for ten seconds and say or do absolutely nothing on TV. That's the equivalent of a year in television time! People will immediately turn it off.*

But Rogers knew the difference. The media's culture of noise is like giving someone meth or cocaine. It overstimulates, lies to your senses, and then something in you weirdly craves it again—even though before you experienced it you never realized you desired it.

The only way to fight something like that is with the anchored, deep, slow presence of silence.

Silence today is so rare, so undervalued, that it is an act of resistance.

Rogers would use that silence strategically. "Silence is the greatest gift we have," he once said.[11] And he fought for that silence *everywhere.*

He even had a ritual in which every meeting, spanning across decades, had to start with silence. He'd instruct his staff and team to take one minute at the beginning of the meeting to think of a person who had a positive impact on their life. And he'd watch the time and tell them when the minute was up.

One year he was invited to the White House for a conference on children's education and television, where he met with Bill Clinton, Hillary Clinton, Al Gore, and the highest-level executives of PBS. And how do you think he started that meeting with some of the most powerful people in the world? With sixty seconds of silence during which they were told to think about someone who had an impact on them.[12]

He did the same thing when he accepted his Lifetime Achievement award at the 1997 Emmys. In the middle of his speech, he took off his watch, told the audience he'd keep the time, and led them in the very same exercise. He was leading not just the audience in the theater, but also the 18,744,000 people watching all over the country in the very same moment. And it was clear from the first second or two, when a few in the audience laughed or howled, they thought maybe he was just joking.

But he was serious.

It was the Emmys and millions were watching. One second of silence could easily lose those millions of viewers.

I particularly love *Esquire*'s account of the moment:

And then he lifted his wrist, and looked at the audience, and looked at his watch, and said softly, "I'll watch the time," and there was, at first, a small whoop from the crowd, a giddy, strangled hiccup of laughter, as people realized that he wasn't kidding, that Mister Rogers was not some convenient eunuch but rather a man, an

authority figure who actually expected them to do what
he asked . . . and so they did. One second, two seconds,
three seconds . . . and now the jaws clenched, and the
bosoms heaved, and the mascara ran, and the tears fell
upon the beglittered gathering like rain leaking down a
crystal chandelier, and Mister Rogers finally looked up
from his watch and said, "May God be with you" to all
his vanquished children.[13]

I wonder how many that night truly experienced their
first minute of intentional, deliberate silence.

That night, Mister Rogers also was reunited with Jeff
Erlanger, a quadriplegic man in a wheelchair who had been
on his show decades before as a kid. Mr. Rogers's gentleness
and tenderness in that moment is honestly one of the most
real and beautiful moments I've ever seen on TV (if you
have a few minutes, go watch it on YouTube). It's when
Mr. Rogers showed himself to be a resister and rebel all over
again.

Here's the truth we have to reckon with: slow or silent
space doesn't mean wasted space—no matter how much our
world tells us it does.

Empty space does not need to always, inherently, be
filled.

It can just *be*.

What would it look like if we were people who reclaimed
spaces of silence as an act of resistance in our daily lives?

The Quietest Place

I grew up in Tacoma, Washington, and if you hop in the car and drive a few hours west around the Puget Sound, you'll end up in Olympic National Park. It's a gorgeous, sprawling area covering most of that left hook you see when you look at Washington State from above. Think *Twilight* and Bella and Edward and you'll begin to picture what it looks like. (The books were set in the tiny town of Forks, Washington, right outside the park.)

There's a particular part of the park called Hoh Rain Forest, informally referred to as one of the seven wonders of Washington State. Lesser known than the Amazon rain forest, it is still quite dramatic in aesthetic and actual rainfall. People always joke that Seattle is the rainy city, which it is—averaging about thirty-six inches of rain per year. But here's the crazy part: the Hoh Rain Forest averages almost that (thirty inches) in rainfall just from *fog and mist moisture*. For actual rainfall it averages fourteen *feet* per year.

And because of that it is one of the most lush and green forests you'll ever walk into (feel free to pop onto Google and look real quick). Moss hangs from virtually every square inch of tree trunk and foliage.

But here's the real reason Hoh Rain Forest is so awesome: If you venture deep into the forest, you might come across a seemingly random tiny red stone. But this stone is not just any stone. It's a marker laid out by ecologist Gordon

Hempton and his friend Fritz to mark the *quietest place in the United States*. It's a marker, a metaphorical stake in the ground claiming ownership and authority.

Oh, and did I mention Fritz is a mannequin doll head rigged with a microphone? Visualize the heads you sometimes see people shooting at FBI training headquarters in all those crime movies and you know what Fritz looks like.

Hempton became interested in searching for the quietest place on earth as part of his research. This led him here.

But he wasn't just set on discovering the quietest place on earth. He is also set on *defending it*. He systematically hikes into the forest on certain days, takes noise readings, and, as he said, "when a noise intrusion occurs, I locate the noise maker, send them a letter and ask for compliance." He continued by saying, "This matter is urgent. It's likely that in 10 years there will be no quiet places left unless we take action."[14]

I think Hempton's work is a great metaphor for our walk with Jesus. There are two steps to carving out this formation.

First, we have to seek silence. To chase after it. Trek into the deep centers of sacred space, looking for where we might find it.

But once we get there?

We have to defend it.

And like Hempton, when a noise intrusion occurs, we need to locate the source and "ask them for compliance." We aren't slaves to the noise. To our phones. To the buzz. To the assault on our senses. We can and should ask—no, better yet demand—compliance.

Our souls are at stake.

And just like any resistance—whether a world revolution, or a coup of an empire—it always, without fail, starts small. With one action. A tiny bit of momentum.

And that's how it is on our journey with Jesus. You aren't going to have a beautiful, serene, three-hour period of silence and solitude right away.

Well, maybe you will! But it surely wasn't that way for me.

It was more like two minutes. And I *itched*.

But I have to resist the need to scratch. I have to stay in it, put one foot in front of the other, and practice. There is a reason it's called a spiritual *practice*—it takes practice. Repetition. Learning and iterating and changing and adapting.

And in that silence you'll find a space where your old self begins to suffocate, your new self begins to be renewed, and the truth of God begins to slowly but surely fill and rewire and recalibrate your new humanness—the self that walked out of the grave with Jesus two thousand years ago to new life, pacing and directing toward the new Jerusalem where all is put back together once and for all.

5.

THE POWER OF NO

Hurry up.

We have to go.

I told you to put on your shoes ten minutes ago!

These are a few phrases I find myself saying. Even more when we are busy or rushed. Yet toddlers have a magical skill of not caring about our concept of being on time. Everyone knows they go at their own pace and have very inefficient ways of doing things.

Of course there are times we have to rush out the door. And of course sometimes we need to make sure we're moving in a speedy fashion. But that shouldn't be the norm.

In fact, after some reflection I realized an arbitrary sense of *hurry* was the force steamrolling us. Or better yet, steamrolling *me*—and I was then steamrolling those I was responsible for. The ones who didn't choose this.

Time stress is a funny feeling. It's a mixture of pressure and franticness and frustration. All rolled up into a tight ball until you feel your soul give way to the idol of hurry. And it's a fairly new phenomenon.

Keeping Time

Modern timekeeping, and modern watches and clocks, have a fascinating history with an enormous impact on our world that tends to get overshadowed by innovations of the same era—like the automobile, the lightbulb, and the telephone.

But the way we got to our concept of timekeeping is quite peculiar. Back in 1657, Christiaan Huygens invented a spring mechanism that finally allowed timekeeping to be fairly accurate, and which allowed the determination of longitude at sea—an enormous breakthrough for the era of navigation.

But still, for the next few hundred years before railroads, time was essentially local. So a local community could have a relatively accurate ability to tell time, thanks to Huygens. But time still wasn't standardized. And that time was usually based on marking midday on the clock (noon) by the moment when the sun was highest in the sky, hence the phrase "high noon."

But, of course, when the sun is highest in the sky depends on where you are in the world. For example, if you are in Philadelphia, you will see the sun at its highest point maybe ten to fifteen minutes after someone in New York.

Local communities would set their clocks to their own observations of the sun, which is fine if you are only coordinating with people in your area. As long as everyone in Philly says it's one o'clock, then that makes it easy for people in Philly to coordinate meetings, work schedules, and whatnot.

But what do you do if everyone in New York is fourteen minutes ahead of Philly, and Boston is three minutes behind that, and Washington, DC, is thirty-five minutes different? It doesn't matter if two people in Philadelphia set a meeting for 1:00 p.m. when someone in New York thinks that same time is 1:14. But it does matter once the world starts getting smaller and more connected.

Once those cities started connecting by train, the time difference became a logistical nightmare. "American railways recognized 75 different local times in 1875; three of those were in Chicago alone."[1] And people started dying. Seriously. Trains had no standard fixed time to go off of, and the absurd math conductors had to do on the fly caused immense confusion and they'd crash into each other and mess up all kinds of things.

That was when, in the UK, railways adopted "railway time," which was based on Greenwich Mean Time, set by the famous observatory in the London borough. The railways ran on one specific time, based on a time from one specific location.

City officials started to see the immense benefit of adopting standardized time across the board. But then people started resisting.

Hard.

India probably saw the most extreme revolution. In what historians call the "battle of the clocks" in 1906, thousands of cotton-mill workers rioted in Bombay. They refused to work and threw rocks at the factories. As the *Atlantic* notes in their telling of the story, "They were protesting the abolition of local time in favor of a new Indian Standard Time based exactly five and a half hours off of the famous Greenwich observatory. This battle went on for fifty years. It wasn't until 1950, three years after their independence as a country, that a single time zone was adopted for the country."

The French felt similarly and adopted standardized time as a country, but refused to set that time by an English observatory. They set ground zero for time in Paris—the greatest city in the world.

Once time was standardized on Greenwich Mean Time, in order for people to have the accurate time, they'd have to go there and look at the time and then set their watches accordingly. Seeing a business opportunity and need to be met, John Henry Belville and his family decided to bring the time to them and created an entire web and network of messengers that would start with one person (usually Belville) attaining the accurate time at the Greenwich observatory and then distributing it from shop to shop and to whoever subscribed to his service.

This service was passed from Belville to his wife and then his daughter Ruth, who alone made these rounds every day for forty-eight years. Not without scandal, though. One afternoon in February 1894, on a day Ruth Belville would normally meet with the Greenwich timekeepers, a bomb went off in the city. It was a French anarchist, who blew his hand off by accident and later died of internal injuries. But it's thought that the bomb was meant for the Greenwich observatory to throw off the world's time, and possibly give the French the new reign as the world's standard timekeeper.[2]

Why does all this matter?

First, our modern concept of time is not what it's always been. Time hasn't been precisely measured, divided, and tracked forever. That's fairly recent.

Second, when that concept of time was first introduced, not everyone was excited.

Third, and most important, a trade happened in the process of gaining that new concept. New inventions always have their benefits, but also their consequences. And it's clear we are better off because of modern timekeeping. But do we really believe we left this deal unscathed?

Since the modern era, and all the innovation that came with it, time has taken on a life of its own. It started to reign over us like a pseudo-god to be bowed down to.

Time is what makes us tick. (Interesting how we see our humanity the same as clocks.) We no longer need Ruth Belville going around town telling us what time it is since time is everywhere. It is a force everyone is revolving around, orbiting around, and submitting to.

Fast-forward to the invention of atomic clocks, which is how we keep accurate time today. An atomic clock measures oscillations in the energy levels of electrons, which is accurate to within a second of one hundred million years. That is so exact it almost sounds absurd.

Our desire to control time, to gain perfect precision, has changed us in more ways than we recognize. At first, our machines operated like "clockwork." Now it's us. Our lives are being formed every day into a more mechanized, robotic, and calculated existence. We are becoming our clocks. As the psalmist said, referring to idols, "Those who make them will be like them, and so will all who trust in them" (115:8).

Tick. Tick. Tick.

The sound of a clock.

But also the sound of most of our hearts. The soundtrack of anxiety and pressure.

We don't eat or sleep when we are hungry or tired anymore—we eat when it's *time* to eat. Sleep when it's *time* to sleep. A day is now an infinite number of moments that can be constantly carved and harnessed and separated for exploitation. So, are we masters of time? Or slaves? That's the dark side to our current timekeeping culture.

It's killing our margin.

In his bestselling book *Margin*, Dr. Richard Swenson defined the term as "the space between our load and our limits."[3] What we are currently carrying is our load, and our capacity to carry that load is our limit.

Sadly most of us have erased that space entirely. We live with zero space between our load and our limit. We are now at our breaking point and have nothing left to give. We are just one small decision away from the load circle and the limit circle overlapping on top of each other perfectly in the Venn diagram of margin. When our limits become our load, that's when we experience burnout and depletion.

But this gets tricky in Christian culture, because we often encourage the idea of being busy to the point of leaving no margin in our lives.

You are doing the Lord's work!
He will fill you up and sustain you!
You need to be doing big things for God!

And that's true, but we were made for more.

Consider margin when it comes to money. The worst financial advice is to spend right up to your means. If someone gave you that financial advice you would not only run as fast as you could away from them, you'd probably warn all your friends to stay away too. You make $3,500 a month? Then make sure your mortgage, utilities, groceries, and other expenses add up to $3,500! No extra. No savings. No margin.

We all know it's terrible advice. Without margin in our finances, we are not free. And I don't mean free to just sit on a pile of cash and be self-indulgent and feel good about ourselves. Margin is meant to first take us out of financial slavery (overleveraged, debt up to our eyeballs, and not living within our means). Once we're there, the margin becomes the space of help and leverage.

We are much nimbler and freer to give and help others—because when we're not slaves, we have freedom. And freedom can be shared.

So why do we not do the same with time? In fact, it seems we aren't just not running as fast as we can and warning our friends about filling their schedules to the max, but instead we encourage it!

If we allocate 100 percent of our time, we have nothing left over—so if something unexpected happens in our days (which we can count on to happen), we are left trying to rush to the next thing. We are now hurrying ourselves—and those around us.

But as my friend John Mark likes to say, "Hurry is violence on the soul."

One of the quickest ways to curb that violence to our own humanity is learn how to say no in a world full of yeses.

Say No

If you're not saying no to good things, you're probably not saying no enough. With the increasing access we have to each other, we have to make sure we're saying no frequently. I personally try to starve my schedule because whenever I feed it, it seems to only grow plumper—needing more and more food the next week and the week after.

For the past few years, I've placed a ruthlessly high value on space and margin. I fight for it relentlessly, which takes an enormous amount of work. I find it weird that people admire others who are extra busy. But honestly, can't everyone do that? Last time I checked, it's easy to fill an entire week. I'm more interested in people who schedule as little as possible, only what is essential and best for their flourishing. *That* takes work. And commitment. Focus. Vision. That's countercultural to the hustle.

Now, some people can make this decision cerebrally and just move on with their lives all prioritized and organized and healthy. That wasn't the case for Alyssa and me.

We had to learn from the great teacher Burnout.

And first spend some time with Master Overwhelm.

We were doing things that seemed great and awesome (which is what hurry feeds on best), but we ended the week feeling unfulfilled. Burned out and a little more on edge. Depleted and wound up.

Even before I was married and had kids, my travel

schedule was a problem. I'd be boarding planes every other week, constantly getting up at 3:00 a.m. for morning flights, getting home at midnight a few days later, then rushing to a morning coffee meeting after a few hours of sleep. Or I'd take a red-eye flight, land in the morning, and have to shower and shave at the airport before hopping on a stage a few hours later. My craziest time was when I flew from Seattle (where I lived at the time) to Florida for a speaking trip, then back to Seattle, but because I had to board another flight a few hours later for another unrelated event, I decided to not even leave the SeaTac airport. I just grabbed a bite to eat and hopped back on my next flight to Missouri, which I probably flew over while flying back to Seattle earlier that day. (Let's just say I've also gotten better at routing flights based on certain locations since then!) I was flying across the world to speak about God and tell people about Jesus and share stories of his healing power and hope and resurrection. Truly life-giving and fulfilling and meaningful work—if only I could have been awake enough to remember it.

After Alyssa and I had children, we faced enormous pressure to do what we thought we were *supposed* to do. We thought we needed to schedule play dates, because our kids need to socialize. We needed to get them in fun activities because, wouldn't they die from boredom if we didn't? We thought we needed to have a family over for dinner at least once a week—to have adult conversations so we wouldn't lose our ability to speak English above a toddler level.

But this gnawing on our souls started to break us. So Alyssa and I started examining our lives with a microscope, asking ourselves, why do we have a full schedule? Why do we think we have to do these things? What stuff is necessary to live and what stuff isn't? What if we prioritize doing *nothing*? Well, I don't call deep and rich and slow relationship building as a family "nothing," but our culture tends to see it that way. Just hang out and get to know each other and love one another and serve each other and walk with God and love your neighbor.

After a few years, we've learned the secret to a calmer life. A lifehack, if you will, to short track your rejection of busyness.

Ready for it?

Make your default answer *no.*

That's it. Without realizing it, most of us make our default answer yes. We specifically believe that time is a more abundant resource in the future than it is now, and we refuse to believe that the time we have today is the same time we will have next week and a year from now. But it is *not* a more abundant resource in the future.[4]

Want to come over for dinner? Yes.

Can you meet for coffee? Yes.

Want to attend this client dinner? Yes.

Can you be the one who brings the snacks to the soccer game? Yes.

Will you lead a small group? Yes.

And it's not just the people who say yes who suffer from the Yes Syndrome. Their family and close friends suffer too. Our individuality is only a small part of a web of relationships and interpersonal communications that affect our work and our day-to-day lives—and the resources we have available.

It has taken practice and rewiring and work, but Alyssa and I have gotten to the place where we say no as our default. We now have to be *convinced* before we say yes to something, which is quite different from needing a good *reason* to say no.

And though we make mistakes occasionally with our default answer, we have more time to truly serve our people. It's not selfish to say no. This is about loving our neighbor better.

So we practice and get really good at saying no. In our world, if we don't learn how to say no, we will lose, simply because we have access to more things than ever before.

We've had to learn to say no in two areas, and both have been different but equally hard journeys.

The first is saying no to the incredibly, awesome, "once in a lifetime" things. And the other is saying no to the daily micro-mundane asks and decisions that eat away at our flourishing like water damage in a house. Slow and steady, and methodical and toxic.

This has been hard. Especially for me. My default position is, "This won't come around again. I *have* to say yes."

For some people, it might be a free paid work trip, but you are having a busy month already. Or it could mean a chance for one of your kids to play for an elite sports team, but your family's energy is already maxed out. These decisions are tempting and hard to turn down. But where we see the most change is in the million little decisions. We get asked over for dinner. We see an ad for a concert we want to go to in town next weekend. We want to sign up for another class at school or church.

Don't buy the lie that a full schedule means productivity or holiness or achievement. This becomes hardest when we are in a position of leadership. If you lead a small group, or you're the president of your student council, or manager of a team at work, or you pastor a church, you'll feel an enormous pull that no other leaders in history have ever had to deal with. It's simple math. The level of access we have to each other is unprecedented. Which means, as the team leader at work, you can receive an e-mail at midnight. You can receive a text marked urgent even if it's not. Your time and attention will be wanted probably more than even a king's a hundred years ago.

We can be called, texted, tagged, snapped, voice memoed, commented to, FaceTimed, DM'd, private messaged, Voxed, e-mailed, WhatsApped, and more anytime. While we're sleeping. When we're on vacation. When we are cooking or cleaning or going to the bathroom. We literally cannot escape someone trying to communicate with us.

And it can be almost anyone. Because we live in a culture of reachability and access where we demand, in nice Christian ways, of course, access at all times to other people.

I e-mailed you yesterday at 11:30 p.m. Why haven't I heard back yet? says the person e-mailing at 6:00 a.m. Uhhhh, probably because I was sleeping.

I'm guilty of this sometimes. I find myself e-mailing someone, and then sometimes texting them saying "just e-mailed you!" which essentially tells them their world and life should revolve around me. Fail.

We often don't get to control how much people ask of our time. Thankfully, though, we do have control over our yes and no.

Is there ever an end point? A finish line? Last time I checked, time is not a replaceable asset. It cannot be bought, rolled over, transferred, or cashed in. It can only be *stewarded* or *wasted*. And by "wasted," I don't mean being lazy. I mean the opposite: wasting time by being busy and over-scheduled. When we treat time the same way we treat the earth—something to exploit, use, and squeeze every last drop of life from—that's *truly* wasting time.

Time is sacred. It's not something in a Petri dish or beaker to be measured and broken apart. We are not in control. Time is something to be submitted to. A table to sit at. Where every moment is holy and beautiful and special.

I've learned to carve up my time so I put my wife and kids first, followed by my work and my craft (writing and creating), my community to whom I'm called to submit and live within, a few select friends, and the margin to be able to listen to God's voice so I don't miss moments he puts in front of me to interact with my neighbors or people at coffee shops.

After that, the clock hits zero. The asset called time is drained. The biggest change in me after embracing this formation is that now I'm simply *willing to admit that my time is limited*. I hold no illusions. I cannot do everything asked of me or everything I'm able to or want to do. In fact, isn't it weird we think that at all? Recognizing that limit, in my opinion, is the first step to what feels like a superpower— much more meaning-focused spiritual work, and much more anchored and loving presence of being.

It's not about being selfish or weird or introverted. It's about creating a life centered around priorities we care about most, making sure they don't fall by the wayside. There simply isn't time for everything. I personally don't feel restrained by that. I come alive because it gives me permission to be all in with my family, Jesus, close friends, my community, and my neighbors.

So if you want me to hop on a call or listen to your new idea, you'll have to tell me which person or thing on my priority list you're more important than, and then maybe we can talk. And that's not even me trying to be sharp. I now view my day as a jar of rocks already full. Rocks represent those things that are important to me. So for your rock to fit in, one *must* come out.

It's okay to believe we have a finite amount of time. It's okay to believe we cannot add anything else to our schedules. We reveal ourselves with our asks—and how we respond to others' asks. Thinking we have all the time in the world is costing us something. Our family. Our sanity. Our health. Our joy. If you don't have enough time to do nothing, then you don't have enough time.

We aren't God. And so we should stop acting like it. Being human means embracing the limits, not trying to cheat them. As David Brooks said, "It's the chains we choose that set us free."[5]

But maybe you're in college, or a medical student, or a single mom working three jobs. Are there exceptions? Is busyness ever okay?

When I think of my mom at certain points of my childhood, I remember that she spent her time wisely. She was a single mom, and single moms are the magicians of the twenty-first century—pulling off things that seem impossible. Growing up on food stamps and welfare and living in government housing, time always felt crunched—an asset draining away from us. But I also remember many times when my mom walked in obedience and said yes to hard decisions that didn't seem logical or right and said no to the hustle that would take her away from me too much.

We have to be careful and give a good, hard assessment of our day-to-day lives. I think there are some seasons when an intense focus is totally appropriate, where a sprint, rather than a marathon, is a worthwhile pursuit to get somewhere. Like working really hard for a year before you get married so you can get out of debt. Making sure you're extra diligent with studying for a set number of years so you can be a doctor. But it must be asked, are you just going to move from that sprint of busyness to another? Do you really need to keep that side hustle? Do you really need to open that Etsy shop that will require a great deal of attention? In other words, what is your busyness attempting to achieve? A bigger house or more social affirmation or some other arbitrary benchmark?

Not many of us recognize—and rarely do we wrestle with—how much we actually love chaos and franticness and busyness. We don't admit that it does something to our soul and we *enjoy it*. It gives us purpose and meaning. We feel needed. We feel important.

And most of all, we implicitly believe the lie that we need to take care of ourselves, because God just might forget about us. But I believe God takes care of his people—even more when they are honoring him and *trusting* his design and Spirit. And he's been doing this since the beginning of the story.

Let It Rest

The Torah *commanded* ancient Israelites to honor *Shmita*, which is a period of time when the people stopped working for one full year to give the land a rest. It happened every seven years. Keep in mind that the land was not just a source of income at this time in history; it was also the foundation of their economy and the way they fed themselves.

God told them to not do anything for an entire year, which, as we know now, is a brilliant principle for soil sustainability and enrichment (something we know as a culture, but still don't do much of, because well, we need to make more stuff!).

My favorite tenant of Shmita is this: "All the produce of the land that grows by itself must be free to all (even animals have equal access), and all loans are to be forgiven, allowing people sunk in debt an opportunity to start over."[6]

It was an enormous, society-wide reset button. This happened even more during the Jubilee, which happened every seven sabbath years and during which even the slaves were set free. They reset the land, the debts, the hierarchy, and the poverty.

When I think of how incredible this would be today—to cease production, let our work rest for a year, and give away what we naturally or accidentally produce for free—I see how implausible it is—and in our system, maybe even unjust. My immediate thought when I consider whether our family could institute a similar model is, *Would that be privileged of us? Would we be able to do it only because of the advantages we have that not everyone else has?*

But clearly the command for Shmita wasn't just for the

well-off—because even the rich were peasant farmers living nomadically on that desert journey to Canaan. Even a tenth of what the poorest person had would have seemed like great wealth. So is it privilege? How did they, living as desert tribes, pull this off?

I honestly don't know. It surely couldn't have been easy. It's an immense risk and vulnerability no matter what century you're living in. Even today among Israelis, the issue is noted but seen as *kashrut*—a subcategory where debates about micro-deviances or ways to observe it are known to miss the heart of the matter. The main debate loses focus as it centers on the rules and how we can not only observe them but also push them without fully breaking them—instead of considering what will happen to our hearts if we are producing without a break, trying to push ourselves to the limit.

But the Shmita wasn't some subcategory to be relegated to debates about various ways to observe the actual law. It's a political statement. A social statement. An act of resistance against busyness, production, our culture's bent to turn us into machines that we are not.

But let us not just throw away or scoff at or write off the Shmita as some impossible archaic law. What if we viewed it as a thread that has been put into the very fabric of existence for the good of our humanness?

Maybe the Shmita is trying to teach us that "people are indeed like the land, in ways that are more obvious in the modern world: For both, when overwork leads to exhaustion, we engineer continued 'vitality' not with true renewal, but with chemicals."[7]

Roundup for the land.

Coffee or energy drinks for us.

That'll do the trick. Or at the very least will mute any cries for help from our souls and lands.

But we can't ignore the most important part. The ancient tradition of a sabbath year was specifically designed to help the orphan and widow, and the marginalized and poor. It was a defense mechanism against poverty and crushing debt and against sinking into a hole you couldn't climb out of. It was an enormous protection to our humanness—financially, spiritually, economically, and physically.

Is our system so broken that if we were to honor this tradition today, a year off would most likely exploit the most vulnerable it was originally intended to protect?

While we might not all be able to take a year off work, the question that haunts me is, do I trust God enough to do it? Do I think he'd actually take care of me if I did it? Isn't that what most of our activity and busyness is about anyway? Trying to hedge our bets, saying we are Christians with our lips, but living as spiritual orphans who need to claw and grasp for every last crumb of provision.

Do we actually believe God will provide? That he can be trusted?

The Freedom of Margin

We can only truly give from margin. Financially. Emotionally. Vocationally.

Purposely living below our means and not buying everything the world says we need—and maybe saying no to an extra car, or a bigger house—leaves margin in our finances. It leaves space. We are spending less than what we have, so we have margin. And when we have margin, we have freedom. Freedom to give, freedom to invest, and freedom from stress.

Same goes with our time.

Don't spend all the time you have. So you can be free and use it to serve.

When I start talking about our family's intense views on time and schedule, it's easy for people to think it's selfish. Or privileged. I've even been asked if I ever let myself be inconvenienced for others. Yes, I do. That's exactly why Alyssa and I keep this meager schedule.

I want to be ruthless about focusing on our priorities in our schedule—*so I can be inconvenienced and actually have time for it.*

To me there is no better way to show someone you love them than to bear an inconvenience of someone else's burden with joy.

But most of us have zero possibility for margin in our schedules, no flexibility for interruptions.

When we read through the Gospels, some of the craziest

stories about Jesus happened because *he let himself be interrupted.* He wasn't in a hurry. What he was on his way to do could wait. He was open to the Spirit's leading.

Most of us schedule the Holy Spirit right out of our calendar, so we don't have space to be ready to serve in the ordinary, mundane, unnoticed ways.

So many love to be busy. Volunteering at a scheduled service project. Taking a mission trip (and never seeing the people again after we leave). Leading a small group (but never seeing any of them the rest of the week).

Our family purposefully says no to those very worthy things during this season of our lives. So we can take dinner to our neighbors on random nights of the week. So the kids and I can write thank-you notes to our firefighters who are stationed two blocks up the street.

Alyssa and I believe passionately that streets matter. That neighborhoods matter. That we are called to live in those places and in those stories. And furthermore, within those oridinary places, we are called to live in ordinary moments as we go through our days, and to specifically and purposely create space so we have time for them. And for the people we live with. And next to. And see over and over again.

I wonder if our busyness with "big things" or "big dreams" or the Great Commission (Jesus' command in Matthew 28:19–20 to go into all the nations and "make disciples") is actually our excuse to not have to know the people who live next door?

When I hear the words *Great Commission*, I immediately think of going out from the call of Jesus to do superhero-type work in a big, loud way. I mean, Jesus himself said "go and make disciples of all nations," right?

But have we somehow forgotten that the person across the hall, and the mailman, and the neighbor, and the barista qualify as people and live in a nation? So why do we have to go do some crazy big thing for God, when the command he gave us can be fulfilled by just being faithful and loving well over and over again?

We probably buy this lie because we don't remind ourselves that the Scriptures, especially the New Testament, are a highlight reel. It's the memorable stories of the early church, compiled to pass on the teachings of Jesus and tell the story of the first-century movement. But it covers just under a hundred years, and it's a pretty tiny book!

Christianity did not become a movement that turned the world upside down because a guy named Paul was crazy, brave, adventurous, and bold and traveled the world to tell others about Jesus. That contributed, sure. But the world got turned upside down because there were thousands of people who loved Jesus—people we will never hear about or whose names we will never know—and they ate dinners with the people around them.

They said hi to their neighbors.

They lived as witnesses in their daily rhythms.

In our family, my work is pretty rhythmic, just as it

probably is for you. I am not able to shift it around much. I have to work during the day—and I enjoy working. But we create space at night and on the weekends to really be open, and we've seen our kids come to life in it. They are less grumpy. Less edgy. More joyful and thoughtful and creative and loving. Because kids can't hide when they are being pressed or squeezed or overcommitted. They wear it right on their faces, usually with tears.

Alyssa and I have discovered that if you faithfully do your work, love your spouse, love your kids, love your neighbor, meet with Jesus, and get in bed on time, burnout tends to disappear. I'm not saying that we don't ever feel exhausted at the end of the week, but we would get through a week and realize, even though we were exhausted, our souls were right. They felt anchored in a way they didn't just a year before. Kind of like that feeling you get when you work out in the yard all day, and you're exhausted, and your legs are hurting, and your hands ache—but because the work was deep and meaningful, you feel *fulfilled*.

We now see that overwhelming sense of drowning as a smoke signal telling us that something needs to change, and it probably has to do with schedules, hurry, busyness, and our hearts. Then we remind ourselves that we're choosing to have a relatively "boring" life full of incredible richness and meaning.

Seneca wrote that one of the more complex and truly confusing things about our human experience is how we treat time. And how we weirdly treat it so much differently than other assets or things under our rule. He said,

> No person would give up even an inch of their estate, and the slightest dispute with a neighbor can mean hell to pay; yet we easily let others encroach on our lives— worse, we often pave the way for those who will take it over. No person hands out their money to passers-by, but to how many do each of us hand out our lives! We're tight-fisted with property and money, yet think too little of wasting time, the one thing about which we should all be the toughest misers. You can only hand so many hours of your day over to other people before there is nothing left.[8]

Even if there is something left, you may have lost the clarity, the energy, and the capacity to do anything with it.

6.

THE DESERT GIFT

There have only been a few times in my life when I've felt truly duped. By God. By society. By culture. And even by my expectations of what I thought something (or someone) should be like. Where I felt left out in the cold and thought, *This isn't supposed to be happening. Not like this.*

One of those moments was when we lost our baby girl, Ellie Grace, in 2017.

Six weeks prior, Alyssa had jumped on the bed with the positive pregnancy test. Baby number three! A family of five. We could officially fill an entire basketball team.

And then I remember when Alyssa painfully said, "I think we lost her."

I knew miscarriage was tough. When our friends who have walked through it had talked about it, I could see it was devastating. But maybe because either they didn't want to dive into the pain too much or they wanted to protect us from it, a story of miscarriage never was more than a few sentences and a sad moment.

But it's not just sad.

It's traumatic. Horrifying. Bloody. Devastating. Surreal.

A life, miraculously woven and conceived in the very heart of God, resting in the womb, dies. Inside another person. You carry life. Then you carry the death.

I felt so shocked by it all I remember thinking, *I have no context for this. I have no context for death.*

Neither Alyssa nor I had ever lost a family member or a close friend. Death had never stared us in the face and breathed on us. Until that moment.

And there's no playbook, especially with two toddlers in the house. Who still need to be fed. Who still need their butts wiped. Who still need baths. And your wife is devastated, passing a dream that no longer holds a heartbeat. In horrible pain emotionally. But no one tells you the physical toll it has on a woman's body. That the body hates death. And convulses and revolts to get rid of it. You almost don't even feel like you have time to process the loss because a three-year-old and a one-year-old have needs. Now.

That's when the curse came close. Put its arm around us and made us intimate friends.

This isn't how it's supposed to be.

Obscurity

We are now two years removed from that moment in our story, and if you follow us online or watch our videos, you had no idea we walked through that pain when it happened.

And that had nothing to do with not being honest. Or authentic. It was about obscurity.

The gift and beauty, and desperate need, of the desert. Of the place of wandering. Alone. The place where God does his best work. Where he meets you most intimately. Where he isn't at fault for the curse, but where he walks with you through it.

Alyssa and I intentionally shared this traumatic experience with only a few close friends and family members. One of the worst and most insidious parts of our overconnected society is we give no margin for Jesus to deal with us in the darkness.

We can't hear him in our trauma or problems or hurt or pain, because we let everyone else speak into it first. We blog about it. We share it on Facebook.

I know not everyone does this, but a lot do—and it's something we have to wrestle with in our overconnected society. But what if your predisposition isn't to share things online? What if it's to be more private and personal? I don't think that makes anyone automatically more "obscure." The dictionary defines *obscurity* as "the state of being unknown, inconspicuous, or unimportant."

And here's the catch.

According to the way of Jesus, that is not a curse.

In fact, we should choose it.

So then, true obscurity is walking through wastelands that are dry, quiet, not applauded, and isolating with Jesus—whatever that wasteland may be.

But I know why most of us have a knee-jerk reaction to overshare or overconnect online. The same reason some of us share our political opinions on Facebook as if that's somehow going to be helpful to another person (if the election of 2016 showed anything, it's that the Internet only polarizes and demonizes these conversations in general). Nuance is usually found over a cup of coffee, not by typing on your iPhone.

It's quick and gives us the feedback we want. Cheap consolation.

But it's not doing the hard work of obscurity. We need to sit in it, believing it's part of the blessing, not the curse.

Because there's only one way to heal and find wholeness. And it can't be found online. At least not in its fullness.

Sharing trauma (or even good things) with the Internet world, while we're in the middle of it, short-circuits the process. It crosses the wires and creates sparks. Loud sparks—noise.

Adoration. Comments like *We love you! We are cheering for you! Oh, I'm so sorry!* But sparks usually mean a bad connection.

What if God wants to speak to us alone? Do we trust he has what it takes? I'm not saying to walk through hardship and trauma alone. You need your support system and community. In fact, I remember how much our close friends and family rallied with us during the miscarriage. Meals. Flowers. The sweetest cards. Prayers written out over text. Help with the kids.

I'm more concerned about the healing part. Sometimes we share too quickly with the world—the Internet, the fringe friends, the public record—before we have truly processed, dealt with it, healed.

The minute we do that, the decibel level becomes too loud, and we can no longer hear Jesus. He gets drowned out. And he's the place of true wholeness and restoration. In a painful but true way. In obscurity.

We need to simply sit with Jesus without pithy prayers. We need to ask for his help and know that he sees us. While healing won't come overnight, we know we aren't going through this alone.

Beloved

We can look to Jesus as the ultimate example of someone who sought out obscurity during his time on earth. He was constantly saying, *Stop. I don't want to be known. Not yet.* He was being pushed to be more public. Pushed to reveal more. And he'd then heal people and say, *Don't tell anyone. It's not my time.*

While the gospel of Matthew starts with Jesus' baptism, temptation in the desert, and good news, it shows us a few peculiar things. First, God in flesh did not start with some grand political speech about hope and change, or a big announcement of, *This is what I'm going to do. I'm here to save everyone! Follow me.* Nope. He started the whole thing with getting wet.

The one person who didn't need to be baptized, got baptized.

Jesus identified with us. He was basically saying, *I'm not just doing this for you, but I'm doing this with you. As one of you. I didn't have to, but I want to.*

As he came up from the water—hair wet, water dripping down his clothes—a booming voice came from heaven: "This is my beloved Son, with whom I am well pleased" (Matt. 3:17 ESV).

My beloved. The apple of Yahweh's eye. Full blessing and adoration and affirmation resting on him as Messiah. Jesus had done nothing Messiah-like yet. No healings. No miracles. No cross.

Yet he already was the beloved.

Author Jonathan Martin put it this way: "When God called Jesus His beloved, Jesus did something truly remarkable: He believed Him."[1]

Jesus was the beloved, not because of anything he'd done yet, but because of who he was loved by. An object of affection. The beloved. With that power and belief and declaration, you'd think he could instantly march right into the city and start shaking things up.

It had to be so strange to everyone who witnessed such a display of power and mystery that Jesus, while sopping wet, turned his back on everyone and just started walking toward the dry, desolate desert.

The Greek word for desert or wilderness in that passage at the beginning of Matthew 4 is *eremos*, which can also be translated as "the desolate place." "The solitary place." Or "the lonely place."

Jesus willingly walked into the lonely place. Why? Because while he knew he was the beloved, obscurity is where it sinks down deep into the bones. It's where it's seared into us permanently—if we will let it.

Do we believe the Spirit can invite us there too? I imagine Jesus on his way to the *eremos* and pausing for a minute to turn around. And he looks at us, motions with his hand to come to him. With a smile on his face. He's asking us to come with him. To the middle of the desert.

The desert is where the red-hot iron of belovedness sears into our soul. It gets pushed from the surface to the depths. It gets put in a place where nothing can snatch it from.

Author John Mark Comer makes the observation, against a very common misconception, that the desert wasn't a place of weakening for Jesus. Too often, we tend to see that story as one where Jesus goes to the desert and gets weaker and weaker, and the Devil preys on that weakness by tempting him in the middle of it. But this only reveals how much we hate and fear the desert—we automatically think going to a lonely, desolate place will be draining and must mean weakness. Instead, the forty days in the desolate place were like that part on any fighting video game when your character is alone and your power meter begins to recharge. He was branding and massaging and marinating the power deep into himself, through the lonely place. And only then, at the end of that time that the Spirit led him to, was he more than ready to face the evil one.[2]

And if Jesus himself needed that order and process, how much more do we?

Yet we want to run right to the job. To the crowd. To the noise. Without recharging first.

Only then, after the desert, the gospel of Matthew says Jesus began his ministry. He went around from town to town saying, "Repent! The kingdom of heaven is near!" This was why he came.

So Matthew set up a narrative where Jesus was baptized, went to the desert, and then began his ministry. And that order is desperately important. Because not many of us actually try to do the same thing.

1. Identity (baptism)
2. Solitary place (desert)
3. What we were created for (kingdom work)

Switch it around or skip a step, and it all crashes and burns. If Jesus just went from desert to ministry and skipped his baptism, he wouldn't have had the power for what it would take to survive the desert. The obscurity.

Have you ever noticed that all three of Jesus' temptations were temptations of identity? Satan knows if he gets us to believe a lie about who we are and what that means, he wins. It's why he starts the temptations with, "If you are the Son of God, then do this."

But that's a lie in itself. You don't prove childhood. You don't prove your last name. You just have it. Belovedness is a right. A gift. Not something to clutch and grasp for. You don't have to hold on tight. You do have to do that with a possession you own. But a right? A last name? You can open your hands freely and your identity isn't going anywhere.

Knowing your belovedness is the only way you can make it in the desert. If Jesus had no baptism, and only desert, who knows what would've happened? With every temptation, when he resisted, that belovedness sunk a tiny bit deeper into his core.

But imagine if Jesus had the baptism but no desert. If he went straight from his baptism to telling the crowds right there at the Jordan that the kingdom of God was close and at hand. Then belovedness would've been drowned out.

God is always speaking to us. But so is the world—and they are usually louder. So without the gift of obscurity, the blessing of the desert, the space of the silence where we can hear the whisper over and over again, where it gets drilled deep into our being, then the job and the ministry will drown it out. Their voices will replace God's.

But if you have baptism, desert (obscurity), and then ministry? Then you're ready for exactly what God has for you.

You've heard you're beloved.

It's been seared into your soul.

And now you bleed wholeness out to others as you walk in your daily life.

Be Boring

A hundred years ago, people might have thought if their crops weren't growing well, they were cursed. Or if their marriage fell apart. Or if a huge sickness hit them.

But for our generation, our curse is much different. It's having to be *ordinary.*

And so we run headlong from where richness and depth are hiding. I don't know another generation so utterly terrified of the thing that can take us there—obscurity, desolation, and ordinariness.

But what if being obscure, to actually welcome it and chase it on some level, gives us the thing we are looking for everywhere else?

Take the phrase "living your best life." It's often accompanied with images of insane ambition and life manipulation and an idolatry of productivity. It's all about building a seven-figure business or trying this new way to hack sleep and morning energy levels, being obsessed with goal-setting, and never saying no to your own dreams and passions. It's mainly about being *noticed*.

I've personally stopped using that phrase entirely, along with all the other cousins of it ("be more productive," "be the best you," "scale your influence," "chase your dreams," and things like that). I've exchanged it for something that's been a lot more life giving. And it's pretty simple. My new life mantra is *be boring*. Seriously. I have it written as a reminder right next to my computer.

Because what our culture defines as boring (or mediocre or wasteful squandering of talent), the Scriptures and the way of Jesus define as quiet, beautiful, faithful.

So I'm going to keep chasing boring because that's the thing that's actually allowing me to live fully. It feels anchored, slow, not anxious, full of joy, and steady, with a peace about it that I think only comes from the quietness of it.

I'll just be over here, saying no thanks to the Internet onslaught of thought leaders telling me to do more and be more and achieve more. Nah bro, I'm good. I don't want to lifehack anything, and I don't want to cheat the work of life.

You can find me chasing a "boring" marriage, and a boring family, a boring work life, and a boring schedule *and loving it*. Because the thing most of us are chasing in all that insane lifehacking culture—a life of meaning and depth and richness—might be found in the boring instead.

And here's where I've had to grapple with this the most: when thinking about our Christian culture and its obsession with doing "big" things for God. What if God doesn't want me to do big things for him? Like, at all? What if he just wants me to talk to him and know him and live an ordinary life where I love him and my neighbors well?

Alyssa and I have been doing this YouTube, social media, online thing as a full-time job now for six years, but I've come to the conclusion that God doesn't care about it as much as he cares about other stuff.

I imagine one day God asking me questions about this life I was given and how I lived it.

Hey Jeff, you know that online thing I gave you and Alyssa? Did you steward it well? Okay, cool. Let's move on.

Hey Jeff, you know that neighbor you've lived next to for eight years? What's his name?

Jeff, you've been going to that coffee shop to work a few times a week for the past few years. Have you ever asked the barista her story?

Jeff, how come every time I tried to meet with you or talk to you, you were more excited to be on your phone, or too busy with your schedule, or doing and not being?

Boring is holy.

Obscure is holy.

Mundane is holy.

Boring is not a sign of the curse, but actually a sign of intimacy. How do you judge the closeness of a friendship to someone? Why do you consider your spouse or your best friend or someone in your family the person you are closest to?

There's a level at which you know each other that just can't be replicated or cheated or short-circuited. It happens slowly, methodically, over time. Building one memory and moment upon another. Over years. Or decades.

If you put me and a stranger in a room, I'd have to be "on," and I'd love getting to know that person. But it's work, because I don't know them.

But with Alyssa? We can sit there next to each other and not speak sometimes. For hours. Our intimacy is so deep. The comfort has been built over years. We know each other. I mean, we *know* each other. To know, and to be known, is what we are all chasing after most of the time anyway.

The longer we get to know someone, and the deeper the intimacy goes, the more boring it gets.

When I first started dating Alyssa, it was the most insanely exhilarating time of my life. I couldn't stop thinking about her, and honestly there was a physical buzz in my body over her. I hummed internally with the magic of the puppy love.

And now?

Not so much.

But guess what?

I love her so much more ferociously and deeply and intimately than ever before.

My love for her as a teenager (we were nineteen when we met) doesn't hold a candle to my intimacy and love for her at thirty.

Boring and ordinary are signs of intimacy to me. So I wonder if in our dislike of those things, we actually are saying no to intimacy too. Shallowness is essentially the king of the day as long as we uphold fast, spectacular, and incredible moments as the markers of true life. Not boring, mundane, faithful love and presence.

Take a look again at Mister Rogers. A dumb and annoying cultural debate, in my opinion, arose toward the end of his life. People critiqued him for creating a "snowflake generation." Essentially because Mister Rogers spent decades telling children they were special and unique, he was to blame for everything wrong in the millennial generation.

Spoiler alert: that's not what Mister Rogers meant by "special and unique," and not what most people who were profoundly affected by him thought he meant either.

The criticism reached peak steam in the early 2000s. And so when he was invited to give the commencement speech at Marquette University in 2001, he made sure to be as clear as possible about what he meant. "You don't ever have to do anything sensational in order to love or to be loved. The real drama of life (that which matters most) is rarely center stage or in the spotlight. In fact, it has nothing to do with IQs and honors and the fancy outsides of life."[3]

You don't have to do anything sensational to be loved.

Or to love.

You don't have to be spectacular to live a full and flourishing existence.

The goal of life is not to be dramatic, noticed, striking, eye-catching, breathtaking, glorious, remarkable, or fantastic.

God already notices you. His eye is caught by you. You take his breath away. You are full of his glory.

God never commands us to chase those things, but he does command us to love him and love our neighbor.

Whenever I've talked about this with others, I've received one consistent pushback: ordinariness dampens or lessens the power of God.

Jesus wasn't a special case. Almost every major figure we know of in the Scriptures had a significant season of obscurity.

By our standards, in fact, many of them look like they wasted their lives.

Moses was the very towering figure in the Old Testament, the most major figure in the Jewish faith. The arbiter and keeper of the Torah and the covenant made at Sinai.

But everything we know Moses for, and everything we celebrate about him, he seemed to barely sneak into his life right at the last minute.

His life seemed wasted and weird by all accounts.

Raised in Pharaoh's household.

Then he killed a man.

Yes, murdered someone.

And then he went out to the wilderness and took care of sheep for four decades.

Imagine if that was your life.

No big things for God.

No seven-figure business by the time you're thirty.

No moving across the world, to travel through Europe and post on Instagram about how incredible your life is at age twenty.

Nope.

One place.

Four decades.

Where no one cared about or knew him, doing nothing special.

Taking care of sheep.

Every day.

Or how about Abraham? The very father of the Jewish faith, and an enormous figure in the Torah. Everything hinged on him and the promise.

He seemingly had wealth and privilege, and was part of a multigenerational line under his father.

He heard from this strange God, different from his father's, who called him to an unknown place, and he did something crazy—he said yes.

And then God said, *Because of your faith and trust, I'm going to make an entire nation out of you. Even though you think you can't have kids, I'm going to put the world back together through you and your family, and your descendants will be like the grains of sand.*

And so he lived in this promise. In radical faith and obedience. Away from everything he once knew. Very much in obscurity.

And at the very end of his life, he had a child named Isaac—because the miracle was so outrageous they couldn't stop laughing (*Isaac* means laughter).

And then what happened?

He died.

And that's it.

Put yourself in Abraham's shoes. God gives you a promise that he is going to make you into a great nation. Bring the blessing and promise and renewal of all things through your line.

And you live for decades with nothing happening.

Then you have one kid and you die.

He didn't get to enjoy the fullness of the promise coming to fruition. But it came true. And because of his willingness to live in obscurity, and relatively "waste" his life under obedience to God, it came true.

He lived his life in obedience, toward a dream he'd never see. Or get to take part in. Or benefit from.

Yet he still did it.

Or take the apostle Paul in the New Testament.

He had a radical experience with the Lord on the road to Damascus. He heard the very voice of Jesus, got knocked off his horse, and went blind. And was told he would be one of the major players for a first-century movement that would turn the world upside down.

And so what did he do?

Did he start preaching? Go around telling people how awesome Jesus is? Did he get back on his horse and race to the city square to preach the fiery and bold good news?

No. He went and spent years in Arabia and then Syria, and it's a time we don't have much information about.

What if God wants us to just love the person two doors down from us? Consistently? For a decade? And that may be all we do in life that's worth anything—at least by God's standards. What if we actually embrace being unknown? Unseen? The hidden place? Why does everything have to be shared or processed out loud?

I know what you're thinking.

Jeff, God doesn't want us to be ordinary! He is big and huge and miraculous and gives us extraordinary moments.

To which I'd say yes and no.

Is God big and huge and miraculous?

Yes.

Does he give us a ton of extraordinary moments in our lives?

I actually don't think so. Or here's a better way to put it: we shouldn't be seeking out those moments, but instead living our lives in the holiness of the ordinary. And if God wants to get our attention with something big, we can trust that he will.

Go back to the example of Moses from the Bible. He was wasting his life away in the desert for forty years. With sheep.

He was a senior citizen. Collecting social security. The point in life where our culture thinks we are essentially done doing anything meaningful. But the only "meaningful" thing we know of him up until his old age is he murdered someone of his own race. A brother of his. After, he silently and quietly lived his life for decades in the desert of obscurity.

Was he wishing to do big things for God? Was he this rubber band pulled back just waiting to be launched at God's word?

No. At least it didn't seem like it.

He was hanging out with sheep, minding his business— not chasing after some big thing to make his life meaningful. Instead, he was faithful and obedient, chasing the meaning of the day in front of him.

Then, all of a sudden, on a random day, he looked left and saw a bush on fire. Yet it wasn't consumed by the fire.

Hmm. That's strange, he must have thought.

Then the bush started talking; God was calling him to lead his people out of slavery.

Moses wasn't angsty, feeling shame over wasting his

life away in an isolated place. Nope. A bush caught fire and started talking to him. God had come looking for him.

But even with those miracles, Moses resisted. Because he wasn't seeking recognition or trying to be extraordinary. He was being faithful in the ordinary, and then when God wanted to get his attention—when Moses was old enough to get a senior discount at Denny's!—he did something remarkable.

So many of us can learn from Moses. And all these biblical characters for that matter. To be present and faithful to the very day in front of us *where we currently are.* We want to do something big. God wants us to be someone who is faithful. What if we just stopped trying to do extraordinary things for God? What if we put our heads down, went about our work, and were faithful in it all? If we did our work with excellence? Loved our friends and neighbors and coworkers? Leaned into the Spirit of God every moment of every day, and were perfectly content to do that same routine of ordinariness every day until we die? What if we were fine with that? What if that type of life was a blessing, not a curse?

I've had to learn this in my own strange and unique way that wouldn't have even been possible a decade ago.

After I graduated from college, I did what many millennials had done—I made a random video and put it on YouTube.

There was no purpose or intentionality or reason or

plan. My friend and I made a video and uploaded it to YouTube. We didn't think past that.

Within twenty-four hours it had gone insane viral. It's strange that a four-minute-and-thirty-two-second video turned my life upside down. Forever.

Some people on the Internet thought it was the best thing ever, while others thought it was the worst thing ever.

It was a surreal experience to go to a website I read every day for news and information and on the front page read an article about how I was extremely wrong and leading millions astray by what I said in my video. Of course, there were positive responses, too, and most people think that those few weeks after the video went viral must have been insanely awesome for me. But it was just the opposite. I hated it. They were some of the hardest weeks of my life. I felt like I was in a pressure cooker of praise, critique, and identity crisis all at once. It was a surreal experience to have so many eyes on me in such a short amount of time. I don't think humans were created to be able to sustain that sheer force of attention.

Thankfully, because of solid mentors and anchors in my life, Alyssa and I were able to walk through the season gracefully. And some cool opportunities came from it. A few months after the video went viral, I was approached by Thomas Nelson and given an opportunity to write a book, which had been a dream of mine my whole life—but it was one of those dreams I didn't even entertain because I saw no viable path to doing it. Then the opportunity fell into my lap because of a video.

And so my first book was published in 2013 and debuted at number three on the *New York Times* bestsellers list and then stayed there for nine weeks. It has sold hundreds of thousands of copies and has been translated into a handful of different languages.

But I was twenty-four and had no context or previous experience. I had no idea that the average book sells three thousand copies, so I thought that was normal.

Until my next book came out.

And that was when the wrestling started. It's surreal to face the reality that your commercial successes are probably behind you. Yet you are still in your twenties. Growing up, I never thought that my career would peak at twenty-four. Most likely, there will never be a video as successful as that first one. And there will never be a book I write as successful as that first one.

What a strange feeling to know that I may (hopefully) write books for the next sixty years and create videos and content for the next few decades, yet by the world's measurement, my greatest achievement is already behind me.

That's when obscurity became real to me, in its own way. Sure, we are still "public" people in one sense. But what if numbers and views and sales aren't the measure of success in Jesus' economy?

What if us being less known, and living in that, walking

in that, wrestling in that, and creating from that, will somehow create more meaningful and effective work?

I am enormously proud of the book you are reading right now. It feels more hard-won and researched and crafted than my first one. It took more work, and I feel that, as with any craft, I've gotten incrementally better at the skill of writing. But what do you do when your first book is the one everyone loves and knows you for?

I even feel a twinge of embarrassment about my first book, because it was literally the first one I ever wrote. Picture your first attempt at anything—painting, car work, sewing—there's usually a level at which it's just not that good, plain and simple. But I also know the world is more complex than that, and I recognize how cool (and strange) it is that God is using something I feel so awkward about. Maybe that's why people read it. It was a book written by a nobody, at an age I probably shouldn't have been writing anyway, yet it somehow touched thousands of people. A crooked stick can still draw a straight line, and that book is a cool reminder of that.

The flip side of this is in how I responded to the success. If I'd set up views or sales or noticeability as the main markers of achievement, I'd be tormented professionally right now. If I wrote books and made videos simply to try to crack the code again, then I'd be chasing my own tail. That's a well of water that never satisfies. Because even if you do crack the code again, it's cheap and hollow and a counterfeit.

The work itself is the blessing. Not the result of the work.

Being faithful in the process is what God wants. Not how it ends up.

Do the work. Love the work. Be faithful.

No matter the results, or accolades, or number of eyeballs on it.

If there is one thing I have learned pretty fiercely, it's that the "work" I do isn't what matters. The goal of following Jesus isn't to do a bunch of things. It's to become a type of person. And there's a place that forms us and molds us deeply if we are willing to go there: The desert. The wasteland. That wasteland looks different to everyone, but it's still a wasteland. To us it was our bedroom six weeks after we found out we had lost our third child. And even typing this right now I can remember how it felt. How painful it was. But the beautiful thing is we didn't go out into the desert alone. There was a Jewish rabbi with wet hair walking a few steps ahead of us. Who invites us to embrace the formation of obscurity. To not resist it, but welcome it. It's a gift. And it's where he is if we want to meet with him.

7.

A DAY OF RESISTANCE

Because I'm *Back to the Future* obsessed (the greatest movie of all time!), I am constantly thinking of times and dates in history I'd use the DeLorean to go back to. Famous moments, riveting moments, interesting moments.

One of those times and places I'd love to go to would be the little town of Swidnik, Poland, on February 5, 1982.

If I hopped out of the DeLorean on the main street, I'd see people grocery shopping, picking up mail, running errands, greeting each other. In other words, everything would be completely normal, except one detail.

Everyone would be carrying their TV.

One guy would be pushing a wheelbarrow with his TV in it.

A mom walking with a stroller with the TV where the baby normally goes.

Others just carrying their TVs with both arms as they do their errands, plopping them down at the counters whenever they stop in to a store and take a break.

This was an enormous and collective act of resistance. A deeply subversive act akin to Daniel and his friends when they said they would not bow in the Old Testament.

In the early 1980s in Poland, there was a clash of the communist authorities (in power since the Second World War) and a popular movement of striking workers called "Solidarity."

Then on December 13, 1981, the authorities attempted to crack down as hard as possible by putting tanks on the streets and stopping Solidarity for good. Hundreds were arrested and dozens were killed.

This only invigorated the movement.

The strikers began to boycott the TV news, which was at that point essentially fiction and propaganda. But a boycott of the news itself didn't hold enough power to embarrass the government or make them relent, so everyone decided to go on an evening walk, exactly at the time the news was on, with their TVs in tow.

And guess what? It worked. It was a quiet, yet very public

way to say, *This whole system is a sham and we want no part in it.* An enormous picture of a community publicly embarrassing the government's propaganda news and simply stating with their walk and TVs in their shopping carts, *None of us care for this or want this and we refuse to watch.*

As one supporter of the movement later said, "If resistance is done by underground activists, it's not you or me but if you see your neighbors taking their TV for a walk, it makes you feel part of something. An aim of dictatorship is to make you feel isolated. Swidnik broke the isolation and built confidence."[1]

It went from being a private and individual act to a public communal act, which opened the floodgates and enabled others to say, *I'm not alone in resisting this government. We are strong.*

At its core, it was an everyday, ordinary act of resistance. And it turned Swidnik and Poland upside down. The "take your TV for a walk out in public right when the news is airing" idea spread throughout the entire country and absolutely infuriated the government. And yet they felt powerless to retaliate, since going for a walk was not a crime.

That's why, when I first heard this story, it immediately shot to the top of my bucket list for DeLorean time travel moments. But second, I couldn't help but think about the similarities this had to the Sabbath.

An ordinary act of resistance.

Because that's what the Sabbath is.

In our Western culture that constantly bends the knee to gods of productivity, work-based identity, and speed, Sabbath comes as a fist in the air every week, saying *no*.

We are not what we do.

We are not what we have.

We are not what we can buy.

The way we topple the empire of workaholic-ness and individualism and burnout speeds is by walking around town every week with our TV of rest under our arms. Put it in your wheelbarrow or your stroller.

Because personally, I don't think there is anything more needed right now in our culture, and simultaneously incredibly misunderstood by religious and nonreligious alike, than the Sabbath.

We need to learn to cease.

We need to learn to stop.

We need to learn to have a day of delight once a week.

We need a day to make sure we are still hearing the proper music.

Dancing in rhythm.

A day to make sure the notes and our lives still align.

Origin Story

When we talk about Sabbath, we are often basing our ideas on some weird cultural or religious picture. But let's go back to the source. Sabbath was created in the beginning. Just not in the way we think.

When we open up the first page of Scripture, we are immediately struck with a deeply beautiful and poetic narrative about origins, which are important (just ask Marvel comics). We need them to properly anchor our understanding and future.

Now some quick backstory. We often miss all the little bread crumbs that set up Genesis as an alternative origin story to the rest of the stories in the ancient Near East. The writer of Genesis was playing off of other themes and ideas at that time, saying a few deeply subversive things.[2]

In other literature of the day, there was the idea that there were many gods. And these gods reigned over various things—the rain, the food supply, birth, and so forth. There wasn't really a concept of one God over *all*. So other creation texts usually center on a specific place, or temple, for that god to reside in.

And when each god's dwelling place was built, two things would happen.

One, an icon or image would be placed in the middle of the temple as a visible representation of this god. Two, the god would be invited to take up residence in the temple. Very much like an inaugural celebration, where it's a grand opening party and you stop the normal work rhythm to celebrate.

The subversive and scandalous thing about Genesis is

that it follows the same framework of the origin stories of its day but completely turns them on their head. It says, yes, God has a temple, but it's not a building—it's the earth. The building of the six days and no physical structure allude to the fact that this God is not regional; he is over all, and the entire earth is his dwelling place.

Then instead of statues made of gold and silver placed in this temple, he makes images of himself wrapped in skin and bone and flesh and places them in the garden. They are the divine icons, placed on earth as physical representations of this God who created *all things*.

And then the final day of creation makes a lot more sense: "By the seventh day God had finished the work he had been doing; so on the seventh day he rested from all his work" (Gen. 2:2).

All has been created and spun into existence. The images have been breathed into. Placed in the temple (earth).

Now what?

Simple—let's party.

It reminds me of July 15, 1999, the day my beloved hometown sports team, the Seattle Mariners, opened up a beautiful new ballpark called Safeco Field. That inaugural game was *set apart*. I still remember the joy and celebration of it all. And seeing Ken Griffey Jr. (the most iconic baseball player of all time) stepping into the batter's box for the first time.

While it was a celebration, it was also an invitation to

fill the building. The new stadium was empty while under construction. For years. But when the inaugural game happened, it was about *filling*—with fans and players, and with the joy and spirit of baseball.

So when we talk about Sabbath, it's about the deep sense of joy and filling and celebration. It's set apart and different. It is the day of rest, but not in the sense of "let's sit there and eat potato chips all day and do nothing."

At its core, Sabbath is an invitation to fill the earth with God's presence. That first Sabbath is when God took up residence in his creation, and so we set apart a day to remember that and ask him to come in a special way again. And again. And again. Every week.

Now imagine how Adam felt on that first Sabbath. Humans were fashioned on the sixth day, which means when Adam first opened his eyes, he was looking at Sabbath and rest.

Sabbath was his baseline. His first moment. His first memory. God's rest and celebration and filling of the earth is Adam's very first moment. And only then could he go work properly and live into the vocation God had given him.

God's perspective was to work, then rest.

Adam's perspective was to know rest and then work.

Too many of us are trying to be like God, when we are Adam. Only when we truly know rest and celebration can we know how to work and to enjoy it. We work from rest, not to get rest.

When I think of Adam and that first day of Sabbath, the word *delight* comes to mind. Sabbath is a day of delight, and it always has been from the echo of the first moment.

But then, in Scripture, the Sabbath disappears for a bit after that. The spirit of it seems to fall away once the curse falls. Work becomes a grind and only produces thorns and thistles. God wants to fill the earth with his presence, but human choice and rebellion are actively pushing him back.

Shalom is broken.

Decay is here.

And now delight is not the default.

Delight has to be fought for. Wrestled for. Wrangled from the very hands of the curse. It's no strange reason why the writer of Hebrews said to "strive to enter that rest" (Heb. 4:11 ESV). It takes work to not work in our culture. It takes effort to cultivate a spirit of rest.

But how do we practically do that?

Holy Days

Our family is pretty Christmas obsessed. If you've ever seen *Christmas with the Kranks*, we are essentially Dan Aykroyd.

We put our Christmas tree up in October.

We start playing Kenny G music in July.

And mint hot cocoa actually never makes its way out of the rotation.

We *love* Christmas.

It's easily the best cultural holiday in America. While other holidays are just one day, Christmas is a *lifestyle*.

The reason I like Christmas so much is that it's one of the only holidays we celebrate as a culture that extends over an entire season and not just one day, and it somehow still has retained a lot of its power to recenter us so we slow down and spend time with family. Christmas is magical.

And that's also why I think Christmas is the closest thing we have in our culture to what the heart of Sabbath truly is. So many of us see Sabbath as a dental appointment— something we might have to do and something we'd all say is good for us, but really isn't that enjoyable (and in many cases dreadful). But it's much more like Christmas—a high point of celebration and delight that isn't perfect by any means, but something that draws us to something greater. I don't think there is a better way to understand Sabbath than to think about it like Christmas (except you get to have mini-Christmases fifty-two times a year—how epic is that?).

First, did you know our word *holiday* comes from the old English version of the word *hali-dægh*, which means "holy day"? And what day is more holy than the Sabbath? One of the Ten Commandments is *observe the Sabbath and keep it holy* (Ex. 20:8). It is literally a commanded day that is holy.

The way we see holidays in America is the heart of holy days and feasts, which is why I always find it funny when one of the first things out of people's mouths when you start talking about Sabbath is, "But do we have to?"

To which the answer is, *of course not!*

But do you have to go to Disneyland?

Do you have to watch *Back to the Future*?

Do you have to eat a three-Michelin-star luxury dinner that someone else paid for?

Of course not. But you also realize you don't ever answer those questions with, "Ugh, do I *have* to?"

You *get* to.

They are treats. Immense blessings.

And I'm sure most have never ever asked that question with Christmas. *Do we* have *to celebrate Christmas this year?*

If my kid were asking me that question, I'd realize they probably don't get what Christmas is or we've done an exceptionally bad job at doing it.

What better invitation than to think a certain holiday (Sabbath) is so important we actually *get* to celebrate it not once a year, but fifty-two times a year?

Let's keep thinking about the similarities between Sabbath and Christmas.

First, many people have the day off of work. (If you're reading this and you've ever had to work on Christmas, thank you. You sacrifice so much for so many of us and we are unbelievably grateful.)

But it's a cultural value to not work on Christmas. In fact, it's one of those rare days you don't expect others to be available. Stuff shuts down. It's a special time of slowing down, to prep many things days in advance so the day can be special, to start the celebration the night before, to have intentional family time, to feast and to celebrate and to rest and to slow down.

As a culture, we have *set apart that day as holy.*

But notice how, in setting it apart as holy, we don't just sit somber all day. We don't prostrate ourselves in prayer the entire twenty-four hours. So it's always frustrating that with any special days that have religious overtones we immediately think boring, burdensome, hard, or too much pressure.

Holy means *party.* Just ask Jesus. His first miracle was at a wedding when he turned water into wine, and he was always describing the kingdom as a feast or celebration.

We don't do a bunch of work on the Sabbath (anyone who has "busied" themselves on Christmas usually regrets it), but we don't veg out and watch football all day (we know this misses the mark too).

Similarly, we observe every single one of the cultural values listed above for Sabbath. Our family has been practicing an intentional Sabbath for over three years now, and I can say unequivocally that it has transformed our family. It has saved us at times.

While some like to say they keep the Sabbath, we know the Sabbath keeps us.

It keeps us grounded, rested, filled. It also keeps us resisting in a countercultural way. We're aware of the hypnotic and alluring pace of our culture that is so anti-thetical to the way of Jesus.

The Sabbath is included in the Ten Commandments, which are about living within God's good design. It's not some arbitrary command; it's simply a fact of the universe. You don't have to, but then your life may not go as well for you as it was designed. Sabbath and work–rest rhythm is the ultimate music. You don't have to dance. But if you sit it out you're saying goodbye to an awful lot of joy and blessing. Standing along the side of the room with your hands folded might feel most comfortable, or least vulnerable, but we also know it isn't very memorable. No one leaves a dance thinking, *Wow, I'm really glad I was afraid to dance all night and just stood against the wall looking at my phone.*

But here's the tricky part: we've inverted our values so much that we've come to believe it will go well for us if we don't Sabbath! I see posts on Instagram from some motivational life coach bragging about how little sleep he gets. It's all about the hustle, he says.

#NeverSleep

You can sleep when you die.

I like to say, if you don't sleep, you *will* die (if not physically, then for sure emotionally, relationally, and spiritually). We honor and worship and value workaholics. Work is our everything. It's one of the core places we find our identity.

While the philosopher Descartes is famous for saying,

"I think, therefore I am," America's mantra is, "I produce, therefore I am."

Think about the Ten Commandments. Are they followed in our culture? Somewhat, I guess. Implicitly.

If I cheat on Alyssa, I'd probably lose everything.

If I kill another person, I'd go to prison.

But if I don't Sabbath? I'd probably have a bigger business, more assets, more money, more accolades, more followers, and more to *show* for my work.

We live in a rigged system that's considered the norm in our culture.

You get rewarded, and rewarded *greatly*, if you don't Sabbath. But just like the coal mining industry, you can extract a lot from the earth in a way that reaps unmeasurable blessing (coal brought levels of power and energy never seen before) only to get to a hundred years later and realize how much it's scorched the earth, depleted it of its resources, and left the earth to die. Short-term gain yet a huge net loss. Thinking work is your identity or some badge of honor is no different.

Shaping the Sabbath

Admittedly, Christmas isn't the perfect analogy for everyone. It can hold baggage from childhood, it can highlight losing someone close to you, or it can be a particularly heavy burden for those who are responsible for the gift buying, the menu planning, and the pressure for it all to be perfect. I've heard more than a few stories from people who wish they could opt out of it all.

But even when we hear stories like that, we know the problem isn't with Christmas. The problem comes from broken relationships or painful choices. The problem is that somehow we started missing the mark. And the reason we want to opt out is precisely because we haven't actually been living in it at all.

The same is true with Sabbath. I've had a few conversations with folks who want to understand the allure of it, but then they immediately tense up as they feel the pressure. *Isn't that just another day to plan and prepare for?*

In some sense, yes. But again, if it constantly feels like that, we can safely say the mark is being missed. Just because it takes extra preparation doesn't mean it's a burden.

It reminds me of our second Christmas with our kids. There were numerous presents under the tree for Kinsley and Kannon from friends and family. We had only made it maybe two minutes before Kinsley started to melt down. Isn't this supposed to be one of the more joyful moments of childhood? It was pretty clear she was overwhelmed. So much stuff. (I don't think adults are much different; we just don't read the signs well. But that's another talk for another day.)

Alyssa and I looked at each other and thought, *Well,*

that didn't work very well. So the next year, we decided to be much more intentional. We set a few ground rules and were creative with shaping the holiday to serve our values instead of the other way around. We started a no-toy policy (they have enough) and asked family and friends to get much more practical things like pajamas or an experience (pass to the aquarium) instead. Or one fun thing we did one year was ask family and friends to get one book for each kid, but not just any book—one their family can't live without, with a special note on the inside cover. And we then added up the presents—Kinsley had six to open. So we started opening one present per day beginning on December 20.

And guess what? It's now one of our family's favorite traditions. It's magical. The kids are beyond thankful for that one gift they open that day. They have more time to experiment with it, enjoy it, use it, show us, and all-around be more joyful and content with it. Instead of overwhelm, we've seen it create a sense of gratitude in the kids. It's way more meaningful.

Why am I telling you this story? Because imagine if Alyssa and I had looked at each other on that first Christmas and said, "This is terrible. Let's cancel Christmas."

That'd be ridiculous. The issue wasn't Christmas. The issue was the situation and how we were going about it. The issue was our feeling freedom to craft an entire day exactly how we wanted it to extract the most life and delight.

So we made changes. And every Christmas we modify

it more. How can we center this holiday on giving not consuming? How can we spend the whole month reminding ourselves of the beautiful expectation of our King Jesus? What are some fun rituals we can build on or create with the kids?

That's Sabbath.

You don't cancel Sabbath because you might have tried really hard to make a perfect day one time and it was terrible. You just move on and realize that was probably too much pressure, or you were sick, or had a bad day before (all normal things), and keep improving on it.

But here's where I think Sabbath is better than the Christmas analogy.

With a weekly Sabbath, you get fifty-two tries a year. And the year after that? Same thing.

Again. Again. Again.

And like any rhythm, you don't start over. Every little thing builds on another.

That's why there might be some incredible Christmas traditions in your family—like walking little gift bags up to the fire station on Christmas morning, or seeing the neighborhood Christmas lights in your PJs. Those traditions are magical not just because you did them once but because you did them over and over, stacking on one another like one huge memory mountain.

It's compound interest. You are playing the long game. You don't get rich off of compound interest because you put in five dollars today. You get rich because you put in five dollars every week for eighty years.

Imagine the richness and depth and meaning and memories you can stack on such an incredible day if you have fifty-two reps a year.

And imagine how much pressure that takes off your shoulders. Because you always have next week. And the week after. And the week after.

A few of our close friends and mentors have been observing and practicing Sabbath for seventeen years! Can you imagine how anchored a life must feel if you party and rest and cease and celebrate every seven days for seventeen years?

Stop trying to be perfect. Start getting reps. And guess what? By going for reps, not perfection, you'll actually get closer to perfection (or better quality anyway).

Professor Jerry Uelsmann learned this as he conducted a fun little experiment with his film photography students at the University of Florida. On the very first day of class he divided the class into two random but evenly numbered groups. He then said one group would be graded entirely on quantity, while the other group would be graded entirely on quality. So one group would concentrate on taking as many pictures as they could, and the other would be more intentional about taking high-quality pictures every time. Essentially one was tasked with a quantity task (the more pictures you take, the better grade you get), and the other was tasked with a quality task (your one best photo is what you will be graded on). They only had to choose one photo to turn in, which would be their grade for the whole class.

At the end of the term it was clear that the best photos hands-down were taken from the quantity group. The students who just went around and took pictures like crazy. No pressure. They experimented. They tested. They learned. While the quality group essentially sat frozen, nitpicking over the idea of a perfect picture rather than just going out and taking the pictures.[3]

Take more photos. Do more reps. And not just because human life is more about process than perfection, but because we get closer to perfection rather than just waiting for perfection.

This is crucial to developing a life of rest. Because this is how life works. As a spiral—moving forward, but always coming back to things that matter.

We need to practice it, as a discipline, because the curse is strong and works to overtake us if we aren't resisting.

It's not a coincidence that the curse shows up in futile and endless work and production. *Make more bricks* is the endless, dronelike call of all of our hearts, and it has been since the earliest stories of the Scriptures. From the story of the tower of Babel, where people wanted to build to reach God himself, all the way to the opening chapter of the Exodus narrative where it says the Egyptians ruthlessly "made their lives bitter with hard service" and made them work as slaves "in mortar and brick" (Ex. 1:14 ESV).

Endless work. The same work. Mindless work. Back-breaking work.

Make more bricks.

Egypt was a taskmaster, beating the Israelites into submission, using them to build an empire.

Are we much different?

Tired, overworked, overspent, overextended, usually from building another person's empire.

A few chapters later in Scripture, as discipline for Moses' resistance, Israel was then tasked with keeping the quota of bricks, but now without straw. *Harder labor. But give us the same results.*

I always wonder what those first few moments in the desert and at Mount Sinai must have been like when God not only invited his people to rest, but commanded it. Over and against Egypt, as a way to say, *I am not that type of taskmaster. I am a covenant God of love and rest and delight.*

But how foreign must that have felt?

To only know slavery.

To only know backbreaking work.

To only know ceaselessly producing more and more bricks.

And then to hear the command, *Stop. Cease. Pause.*

We can easily romanticize that and think it must have felt good and full of life. And I'm sure it did for the people of God.

But I'm also sure they must have itched just a little.

Buzzed just a little. Tapped their leg on that first Sabbath, almost longing to make bricks because that's all their muscles and hearts and brains knew to do.

I know that because that's how it still is today. With us. In our family and in our pursuit of Sabbath.

We love Sabbath. We practice it. We live in it. We delight in it.

And I still itch.

Usually around the eighteenth hour I start itching to do something. To be important. To turn my phone back on and see what is really happening. What I missed.

Why do I start itching for my phone like clockwork on Saturday afternoons after it's been off for a day or so?

In short, I'm captured by it.

We long for things we love.

When I'm away from Alyssa, I long for her.

It's not just about attention, but affection. And it's that battle that is the true fight of Sabbath. And what makes the Sabbath a day of resistance. Where we put our stake in the ground and say, *I am not what I do.*

And man, it's hard when I have a deadline or an e-mail that feels urgent. It's hard to believe that it can wait. It is not that important. To believe that I could indulge in it but risk a part of my soul.

Because that's the journey God is taking us all on. The same journey he took his people on in the desert. He rescued them from slavery. Brought them out into the desert. Spoke tenderly to them. Gave them a new way of life—no longer brick makers but Yahweh worshipers. It was no longer about doing, but being. Not about activity, but identity. But let's not forget how many times the Israelites wanted to go back after Moses had led them out of slavery. They even said it was better in Egypt than with Yahweh in the desert!

Why do we think we are any different?

We need to steadily put one foot in front of the other and learn how to dance with our Creator in the desert, where he makes streams of water and shalom and rest flow to us and through us, in renewal and refreshment. Where he teaches us to be a new people. Where he gives us a new way of life.

8.

EMPATHY

Daryl Davis is a blues musician. And he's black.

That matters because his "hobby," as he calls it, is to actively seek out white supremacists, including current and former Ku Klux Klan members. Over three decades while traveling as a musician, he says he's "accidentally" persuaded around two hundred of them to completely abandon the Ku Klux Klan and has deconverted them from their racism.

He says he doesn't set out to convert anyone, get in any arguments, or even talk much at all. He simply listens and empathizes and only asks one question.

How can you hate me when you don't even know me?

He then demands, through love and a shared table, that they look at him eye to eye and empathize with him.

We can't caricature someone who has come close—in conversation or at our dinner table. And it's awfully hard to hate someone that way too.

That's what empathy does. It draws us close when we'd rather be far. It pulls us in when we don't want to care. It focuses when we'd rather not pay attention.

It's the heartbeat of us as humans—storytelling. Understanding and listening to other people's stories.

Now, this isn't to say everyone's point of view is equally valid or worthy. In fact, in many ways it's the opposite. Daryl was not obligated to enter into so many of those Ku Klux Klan members' lives. But he decided to. Out of love.

We are not forced. The minute we are, it's no longer love.

But Daryl was willing to. And that's a skill or superpower we all need to recover. Because the Internet wants to pull us further apart. So we need the thing that pulls us closer together—empathy.

Building a Society

A few decades before the American Revolution, a peculiar trend started to show up among many Americans. The promise of the West during that time was that you were living in history. *This* is how humanity and government and community should be structured, because it's far superior to anything else. The prevailing sentiment was pride in finally achieving the zenith of what we had worked thousands of years for: civilization. This is as good as it gets.

But then something strange started to happen. People who were outside that culture (namely, Native Americans) didn't see the Western American way as that attractive and the Western American people started to get drawn into Native American life.

Benjamin Franklin started to notice this and wrote to a friend in 1753: "When an Indian child has been brought up among us, taught our language, and habituated to our customs, yet if he goes to see his relations and make one Indian ramble with them, there is no persuading him to ever return."[1]

Apparently Native Americans didn't think Western culture was as awesome as we were claiming. It had been founded on the promise that this moment was the zenith of all of history, and taking us into a new age, but outsiders continually said, *Nah, I'm good.*

Franklin also noticed the opposite problem: "Those ransomed by their friends, and treated with all imaginable tenderness to prevail with them to stay among the English, yet in a short time they become disgusted with our manner of life and take the first good opportunity to escaping again into the woods."[2]

English people would literally be captured by Native Americans, and if they were ever recovered or ransomed back into English society, there was a noticeable pattern of them hating and being disgusted by Western life. They wanted to go back to tribal life.

And we are not just talking Stockholm syndrome. Children didn't want to return to their original families. Adults wished to stay after they were captured. Some men were never captured but simply walked off into the treeline and gave up on the West, never to come home again. As Sebastian Junger, in his brilliant book *Tribe*, said, "The frontier was full of men who joined Indian tribes, married Indian women, and lived their lives completely outside of western civilization."[3]

What do you do when you're building a society greater than anything the world has ever seen and there are people who don't want it? Can you really say it's that great?

Junger notes that the reluctance for groups of white men to leave their tribes even when released "raised awkward questions about the superiority of western society."[4] It's an indictment right on its face. If this new democracy and Western world and worldview are the best thing since sliced bread, why do so many reject it?

While we can find thousands of examples of this happening in the historical record, it seemed not even one Native American wished to stay within Western civilization.[5]

This is because we were created for tribes. No matter how hard we try to escape them, we find them somewhere—in either a cheap or authentic way.

But in the West, the individualized self is the highest goal in our society.

And what usually stands in the way of the full realization of the self?

Other people.

Other groups.

Other tribes.

So we throw them off.

We detach from our neighborhoods. We move frequently, never rooted, and never talking to the person who lives fifty feet from us.

We detach from our jobs. Find me someone of the millennial generation who actually thinks it's a good idea to have the same job for forty years, working alongside the same people.

We detach from religion. Because who needs ancient meaning and anchoring in our Creator who is full of love and grace? So archaic, right? I'd rather be "free" and give my allegiance to something much more trivial and ruthless, like pleasure seeking or my workplace identity.

And what do we do instead?

We start trying to find people who look like us, talk like us, dress like us, act like us, and believe what we believe.

Here's the problem: We live in a society where for

the first time, we can fully achieve that. There aren't any roadblocks.

You're a progressive liberal white person? Well, get out of Oklahoma City and move to Seattle. And if you are that person with a little extra dash of spunk? Move to Portland.

You like guns and the American flag? Move to Texas.

You think Republicans are all that's wrong in the world and an evil to be rid of, then how about following only Democratic voices on Twitter, Facebook, and Instagram?

In short, we hate each other and want more of ourselves. So we gather around, or move toward, or follow online people who are like us, which in a weird way is actually just worshiping ourselves. We believe we are God and only want to be surrounded by others created in our image.

Before the Internet and detachment of communities, jobs, and religion, we might have had certain beliefs, but we couldn't escape the people we didn't like or who we disagreed with. They were our managers at work. Our friends at church. Our neighbors.

But if we've retreated to our echo chambers, we need to realize it's killing us. As much as we want to escape tribes, we only create a vacuum where life isn't as sustainable or rich or meaningful.

We leave the tribes that actually cost us something. Instead of attaching to each other, we find pseudotribes that give us a blessing without the hard work or responsibility it used to take to get us there.

The Empathy Killer

I like to call Facebook the Empathy Killing Machine, or EKM for short, because of all the dehumanization that happens there. It's a perfect blend of desensitization and information overload. I can scroll past a story of the horrific atrocities happening to children and adults in Syria right now, and then to some weird plastic body wrap thing my friend is selling.

It's jarring to say the least.

But it's also an exercise in distraction. It stirs up false empathy in a way that makes us feel satisfied. I mean, how many videos of dogs finding their owners after a flood, Marines surprising their kids, or brand-new cars being given to people who can't afford them do we need before we realize we might be wasting our emotion on Internet moments instead of where it's really needed?

It's not only desensitizing; it's also dehumanizing.

Our entire essence is wrapped up into a little pixelated profile picture. We only like things we want to like and curate things we want to see—further creating and hardening our ability to never have to see things we don't want to see or disagree with.

And when we do?

We go on the attack.

If I post something about partnering with a nonprofit organization to help children in underdeveloped countries get access to clean water, a good education, and proper medical care, guess what? Crickets. No comments or likes.

But if I post about how our current culture sees children as consumption and draining agents, when only a hundred years ago that was never the case, then the post goes crazy—even if it was written in kindness and gentleness. People reply in an offended tone, "*Well you just wait a minute right there!*"

Why is that?

Maybe because no one is sensitive about children overseas. But if someone talks about our own children? If someone's post gives people something to consider about their own family, something that is empirically obvious and researchable? People are deeply sensitive on that front.

But here's the more insidious and harmful thing happening under the surface: the very model technology companies use to measure where we spend our time is toxic. It is built on the premise of only promoting posts that get *strong reactions*. Facebook doesn't care if those posts include misinformation or wrong or hurtful content. Facebook just cares that it gets a visceral, emotional response.

We are preyed on by corporations who sometimes understand our biology and creaturely-ness more than churches do.

We are story creatures. We are emotional beings. We are moved by how we *feel* about something whether we like it or not.

And that impulse has been latched on to so a select few companies can make trillions of dollars.

An emotional reaction from us means engagement. And engagement means eyeballs and attention. And eyeballs and attention are the currency of the world.

But in letting our eyeballs be bought, we are giving over our empathy at the same time. We are changing, and something is changing in us.

And here's the unprecedented thing about our culture today that has to be reckoned with.

Everything you read and see online is curated from an algorithm based on exactly what you want to see. Not on what someone else sees. That's why you see different news stories on Facebook than your friend. You get on your news app and see a different front page than your parents.

Not long ago, the newspaper was the primary source of news, and it was delivered to most people's doorsteps every day. Imagine getting up in the morning, getting your coffee, heading to the porch, and finding a newspaper—but it's different from the one your next-door neighbor got. And then imagine both of your newspapers are different from the person's across the street. Then imagine a block over, another neighbor got a newspaper that seems to directly contradict all the news you read in yours that morning.

And that's how information and news works in our Internet age.

It's a pretty simple formula—because our eyes are worth

money, Internet search engines want to create products and services that keep our attention. And to keep us there longer, they give us what we want to see. We have computers sophisticated enough to do exactly that for every person on the planet.

We live in a culture drunk on choice, preference, wants, and desires. We want what we want, exactly how we want it, when we want it.

We don't have to submit to what the actual news is. We can just go find the "news" we want.

This is gasoline on the fire because it breaks us up into tiny tribes, and then we yell at each other online.

Since we're not engaging with actual people but with technology, we don't have to disagree in a thoughtful and relationship-keeping way. Because the relationship doesn't matter, the disagreement can be toxic, mean, and harsh.

It's clear: it's a gloves-off culture we are now living in, which is pretty much the opposite of empathy.

Us Versus Them

Back in 1947, the first television camera was placed in the House chamber of the United States Congress. In 1979, the first televised proceedings were shown on C-SPAN and PBS. It was the first time in history people could watch what was actually going on in Congress with their own eyes, on their own TV.

These televised proceedings happened without much fanfare. The congresspeople didn't really bat an eye.

Except for one freshly minted congressman who saw it differently—Newt Gingrich. He started invoking a special order—a "rule in the House that at the close of business and any day, any member can claim the floor for any reason they want for pretty much any amount of time they want."[6] So he started claiming these special orders at 10:00 p.m. Or 11:00 p.m. When literally no one else was in the chamber.

All the other members of the House were at home. Sleeping. Working late. Having drinks with friends.

But Gingrich wasn't speaking to the House members. He was speaking to America.

Before this, the House was consumed with extremely tedious, boring, and dry material. *Congressmen and women, will you please direct your attention to chart A showing the correlation between farm subsidies and the implications for our budget?*

Gingrich, however, started talking to America—not about charts but about politics and anger and frustration and the corruption of the Democratic Party. It was a late-night political pundit show before those were a thing.

It was us versus them.

And in many ways it worked. Gingrich (not by himself, but certainly because of his vision and rhetoric) was able to boot the previous Speaker of the House on ethics charges (he resigned), regain control of the House as a Republican majority that had been Democratic for more than two decades, and later himself become Speaker of the House. He started a coup and achieved his goals.

By stirring up emotion, not reason. By pandering to fear, not love. By not working with the other side, but making sure everyone knew that to win you have to hate the other side.[7]

And this is how we arrived at our current political climate. Where there's no need to play nice or be coy because it's an all-out war.

Take Frank Rich, a prominent leftist essayist, and his article in *New York Magazine* titled "No Sympathy for the Hillbilly." It's essentially an argument against being nice or kind or empathetic and saying, if you are angry at the people who voted for Trump, hang on to that anger and "weaponize" it.

It's a classic us-versus-them manifesto. Telling us essentially, "We will never get to where we want until we get rid of—or at least defeat—those we don't like."

With each passing year, we are asking politics to carry even more of our core identity.

We are asking it to create more meaning.

Asking it to give us a sense of belonging.

We are asking for more return on the investment, but we are playing a backward game. As Andrew Sullivan so brilliantly noted, we are asking politics to do too much. We are created for tribes, but none of us realize that we're asking politics to fill that gap.

Successful modern democracies do not abolish this feeling; they co-opt it. Healthy tribalism endures in civil society in benign and overlapping ways. We find a sense of belonging, of unconditional pride, in our neighborhood and community; in our ethnic and social identities and their rituals; among our fellow enthusiasts. There are hip-hop and country-music tribes; bros; nerds; Wasps; Dead Heads and Packers fans; Facebook groups. (Yes, technology upends some tribes and enables new ones.) And then, most critically, there is the *Über*-tribe that constitutes the nation-state, a megatribe that unites a country around shared national rituals, symbols, music, history, mythology, and events, that forms the core unit of belonging that makes a national democracy possible.

None of this is a problem. Tribalism only destabilizes a democracy when it calcifies into something bigger and more intense than our smaller, multiple loyalties; when it rivals our attachment to the nation as a whole; and when it turns rival tribes into enemies. And the most significant fact about American tribalism today is that all three of these characteristics now apply to our political parties, corrupting and even threatening our system of government.[8]

It's snowballing toward overhyped tribalism and unmeasurable and catastrophic societal effects. We need to be the people of God who provide a prophetic witness to our culture, an alternative to the people who just jump into the comment section of your aunt's post and to give snarky, sarcastic, rude, judgmental, unempathetic, and uncompassionate opinions—things I see from Christians every single day on the Internet, things that are frankly unbecoming of us as the people of God. We do know that when Jesus said in Matthew 12:36 that we will give an account for everything we ever say, he meant what we type and post on the Internet too, right?

But we drink the same poison, so all we can offer is the same kind of toxic communication.

What We Mean

The way most people communicate online today is toxic and dehumanizing. It's honestly killing many of us from the inside out. And I think there's one question that can really save us all right now. It's so simple, but it changes everything. Or at least it has worked for me over the years.

You ready for it?

It's really world-changing, so watch out.

Before going crazy and going on attack mode, ask:

"Well, what do you mean by that?"

It's sad, but online platforms are clearly set up to reward sharper and more polarizing posts. So as followers of Jesus we especially have to lean into the tension and give people the most gracious interpretation of their words. And maybe this is because I felt so shamed and hurt seven years ago over a video where 90 percent of the very intense critique would have not needed to be written if they would have first asked, "Hey, Jeff, what do you mean by 'religion'?"

For example, when someone asks me if I am a feminist, I like to ask them, "What do you mean by that?" Because the answer is actually a hard yes or a hard no depending on what they say. Or if someone asks me if I'm political, I ask, "What do you mean by that?" If they say giving full allegiance to a political party in a borderline idolatrous way, the answer is no. But if they say and understand that being a Christian is inherently political because Jesus is King and cares for the city deeply (the actual definition of politics comes from the Greek word *polis*, which means "of the city") and all earthly powers must submit to him, and that he deeply messes with people's power structures, which was why he was crucified, then the answer is yes.

Trying to understand each other should be normal, but sadly it is becoming almost a superpower in our culture to have the ability to really lean into someone's point of view and gain true understanding and nuance first before we respond. Instead, Internet culture rewards straw-man fallacies times a million, but as followers of Jesus, we really have to check ourselves in how we communicate with others, because frankly we are killing ourselves over it.

So why is tribalism so appealing?

I think it's pretty simple.

It's easy and doesn't take a lot of work.

Fear Frenzy

You've probably heard that fear of public speaking is one of the greatest fears in our society. That doesn't come from some random backwoods survey. It actually originated with Chapman University and their now famous "Survey of American Fears," which started in 2014.

Among others that year were walking alone at night, being victim of identity theft, and being the victim of a random mass shooting.

But those are no longer people's greatest fears. It's fascinating how drastically those fears have changed in just a few years.

For two years in a row, want to guess what the number one fear has been among surveyed Americans?

Coming in at a whopping 74 percent of those surveyed, saying they were afraid or very afraid, was the fear of "corrupt government officials."[9]

In fact the three top fears for 2017 were corrupt government officials, health-care concerns, and pollution of the environment (and the top ten included the US being involved in another war, North Korea, and another financial collapse).

All highly political and media-centric stories.

The professor in charge of the survey noted, "We are beginning to see trends that people tend to fear what they are exposed to in the media. Many of the top 10 fears this year can be directly correlated to the top media stories of the past year."[10]

Basically, the stories we see and hear are whipping us up into a frenzy, fanning the flames of fear. How big will the fire get before it consumes us all?

No wonder politics has become so divisive and harsh; our greatest collective fears are wrapped up in it. Fear is the greatest motivator there is. It's what drives us. It is the tick in the clock of our hearts and minds.

I always find it compelling that the apostle John, in his famous section on love in the New Testament, never once mentioned hate. If we were asked for a knee-jerk reaction to the opposite of love, what would almost all of us say?

Hate.

But that's not correct. Fear is the thing under the soil giving the hate life and growth.

Fear is a deeper, much more insidious, motivator.

And almost every atrocity in the twentieth century—from the holocaust to the Rwandan genocide—can be traced back to a deeply held fear that then was stoked into hate.

We fear *the other*.

Whatever the other is for you. White. Black. Republican. Democrat. Sunni. Shiite. Jew. German. Christian. Atheist.

But we have to dive head first into that dark and muddy part of our heart. Not put it away. Not shy away from it. Not run from it.

What's down there at the depths?

What are we truly afraid of?

That someone is going to take something from us?

That we are going to lose something?

As a Christian, I think of our current climate where many evangelical leaders show blind allegiance and idolatrous bowing to the empire of Trump and political power.

But is political power really what we want?

Especially as followers of Jesus we have to ask what we want, and we have to ask what we are afraid of.

Because here's the thing I think makes us distinct from others: We have absolutely nothing to fear. Not even death itself.[11] *What can the world or others do to us?* And this is why *actually following the way of Jesus* is so critical compared to just extracting Christian truths to adapt to our lives.

If we consider how Jesus actually walked and look at his ethos as he went about his life, we find someone who was afraid of no one and no thing. And this prevented knee-jerk reactions. Prevented him from picking up a sword and taking down Rome.

And it made it possible for empathy to radiate from his very being. Because there was actually room for it. There was nothing to be afraid of. All authority on heaven and earth had been given to him. He had legions of angels at his disposal. He had divine representation and authority in himself.

And yet, *he chose to willingly die for others—namely, his enemies.*

And that changed the world.

What's interesting is if Jesus would have actually taken up the sword and tried to jockey for power or take things into his own hands, there'd be no Christianity. There might have been a flash in the pan. But no movement that turned the world upside down, that's for sure.

Only love can do that. Sacrificial, bloody, enemy-love.

A political party isn't our enemy. A certain political policy isn't our enemy. A person with a different experience, skin color, or way of life from ours isn't our enemy.

Sin is the enemy.

And there's only one thing that has the power to quench the giant that is sin.

That is that person and piece of wood raised up outside the city two thousand years ago.

Dying for enemies.

Grasping for nothing.

That breaks cycles. Chains. And powers.

If you're a follower of Jesus and you're reading this, ask yourself, why are you afraid? Look at where you get the angriest or most uptight and I bet you'll find your greatest fear. What would it look like to lay down your fears, hate, and weapons and pick up enemy-love instead? Empathy not as some twenty-first-century value that's easy, but the very basis of hard-won, practiced enemy-love. In Jesus' worst moment, it's no coincidence that empathy showed up.

"Father, forgive them, for they do not know what they are doing" (Luke 23:34).

This is our singular witness as followers of Jesus. That we are afraid of nothing and have nothing to lose, because our very King looked death in the face and defeated it. Death has lost its sting.

And so we become part of a tradition that has shown this singular witness of enemy-love for thousands of years—from Polycarp, the famous church leader who in AD 155 was told soldiers were coming to arrest and execute him for his faith and decided to make them dinner, to Martin Luther King Jr. and his imprisonment, beatings, and eventual assassination for marching year after year under the banner of enemy-love.

And here's what I've realized about this in my own heart.

The difference between fear and enemy-love is a difference of franticness and peace.

Fear is frantic.

Fear goes at a speed love does not.[12]

Fear is fast. Fear is frantic. Fear is distracted.

But love?

Goes about three miles per hour.

Seriously. Three miles per hour is the average speed of someone who is walking purposefully yet gracefully.

And for some reason I see Jesus walking that speed as well. Just the right speed to intentionally take him somewhere. But also the right speed to be perfectly interrupted.

Have you ever noticed how a lot of Jesus' miracles were not a part of his plan? They happened *on his way somewhere else*.

You have to go at a pace that can be interrupted. That can be responsive to the moment in front of you.

And when you are going at a pace that is in step with our Lord, don't be surprised if empathy and enemy-love show up.

Because you can't love someone when you are hustling. And you can't love someone when you're going fast. (Just ask my kids if I'm loving them well when I try to get out the door in two seconds when we are late.)

But when you say no to the hustle?

You can be stopped. You can step into the holy moment of grace. Jesus did it.

He felt other people's pain. He leaned into their space. He understood their hurt. He waited and didn't hustle past.

He loved.

EPILOGUE

WHERE DO WE GO FROM HERE?

I think we can learn a great deal from the now extinct word *snoutfair*.

You've probably never heard of that word (which means "a person with a handsome countenance," by the way, and I've told Alyssa it should be the only descriptor she uses for me from now on). The word became obsolete and was removed from the dictionary.

Why does this word matter?

Because I think the word *faithfulness* is well on its way to die the same death as the word *snoutfair*.

A hundred years from now, someone might say the word *faithfulness* and some will chuckle and others will say, "What's that?"

We just don't care for the word, or the practice, or the value anymore. But if this book is anything, it's an all-out plea to recover it. There's no greater antidote to the poison of hustle than diving headfirst into what the word *faithfulness* means.

The hustle won't give us what we truly want. Quiet, steady, measured, consistent faithfulness—it's a gift. It's what we are all looking for anyway. It's time we stop fearing it so much.

Be faithful to our work and do the same job for fifty years with joy? Nah. I'd rather bounce around every few years, especially if there's any workplace conflict, and just blame it on someone else.

Be faithful to a marriage? No thanks. If it gets tough, I'll just end it and move on. My individual happiness is more important.

Be faithful to a city or location? That's okay. I'd rather not know a particular neighborhood for the long haul. I'll move right when it starts feeling vulnerable or mundane. When the place I live stops being Instagrammable? I'll just move to the neighborhood or city that is. (Americans move more in their lifetime, by far, than almost anyone else in other countries. Transience isn't just a behavior; it's an actual value we highly regard.[1])

I think we hate faithfulness so much because at its root it's obscurity and ordinariness, which is the biggest cultural curse we have today.

There is a certain paradox in making changes and choices that don't seem to have obvious benefits.

It'll feel uncomfortable to resist technological advancements.

To rethink how we communicate.

To question the noise all around us.

To not hustle to get ahead, but rest to be human.

The more I root myself in a place, in a job, in mundane repetition of my life with love, the more I find joy springing up all over the place. Not to mention how the pressure subsides. Is there any bigger reason for our cultural anxiety than the pressure to have a booming career, our goals all written and achieved, an efficient life, a nice house, money, and meaning all by age nineteen?

And what's my actual goal in life? What am I trying to do here?

Keep my head down. Love those in front of me and around me. Honor the process and the present. And be face to face with my Father when I die and hear, *Well done, my good and faithful servant.*

Not, *Well accomplished, my busy and hustled servant.*

Well done.

Faithful.

If we want to get there, we have to actively resist the myriad voices and influences that subtly hypnotize us into a busier, noisier, more hustled lifestyle.

Say, *No, that's not the way of Jesus.*

That's not the speed of Jesus.
That's not the cadence of Jesus.
To hell with the hustle.
I'll take him instead.

ACKNOWLEDGMENTS

One thing a lot of folks who spend ten-plus bucks on a book and read it in a few sittings don't tend to realize is how much a labor of love a published book is and how many years and people it took to get it into their hands. To help give a few more faces and names to your imagination, know that without the people below, this book wouldn't be in your hands (with you hopefully having enjoyed it! If not, blame the people below, not me, obviously).

Alyssa and the kids—thank you for hearing me blab about this idea and all its different stages (just an idea, to "what about this?" to the handful of rough drafts before the final). We truly are a team, and I'm thankful for how much you and the kids enable me to step into this calling and vocation of writing by all your support and teamwork!

Curtis and Mike and the entire Yates team—you guys are beyond gracious to me. Thank you for championing my ideas and projects I care about like this. I wouldn't be a writer or do this without you guys, and it's a joy to count you all as family!

Angela—this book would honestly be so bad and so all over the place without your genius Yoda-level skills of shaping, editing, shutting down my terrible ideas (thank you!), and more. It's an honor to work with you, and Alyssa and I are so thankful for your friendship!

The Nelson Team—y'all are like family at this point. Four books and seven years later, I can't believe I get to work with such a world-class team that is creating and publishing some of the best and biggest books out there! It's such an honor to have worked with you guys over the years to now forming friendships and feeling like family with you all. To Jenny, Janene, Brian, Karen, Tim, Jamie, Rachel, Kathie, Jamekra, and more. You guys are THE BEST!

To my mom—thanks for being the best mom ever. You truly have impacted me so much over the years, and I wouldn't be who I am today without you. You taught me how to work hard, honor others, and live with integrity by your example, and for that I'm indebted and grateful. Love you!

To our Maui community—you know who you are! To listening to me work out this idea at late-night dinners and over s'mores in our backyard, thank you for praying for us, supporting us, and always cheering us on!

NOTES

A Time to Resist

1. One quick note about the word *hustle*. When I say the word *hustle* in this book, I do not mean *hustle* as in working hard, diligently, and with focus (i.e., your coach telling you to hustle for the ball, which is a good thing!). I mean *hustle* as it has culturally been adapted to mean in our online conversational lexicon: a mind-set of do more, grind more, be more, accomplish more, #neversleep, and all that the word tends to tell us to do right now.

2. Quoted in Derek Thompson, "Workism Is Making Americans Miserable," *Atlantic*, February 24, 2019, https://www.the atlantic.com/ideas/archive/2019/02/religion-workism-making -americans-miserable/583441/.

3. Thompson, "Workism," *Atlantic*. This article is very helpful in tracing this problem and phenomenon over the last hundred or so years. I was already bouncing around a lot of these ideas and thinking through them when I came across Thompson's article during the first round of edits on this book. The article is worth a read and inspired a good chunk of this introduction.

4. Amy Adkins and Brandon Rigoni, "Paycheck or Purpose: What Drives Millennials," Gallup, June 1, 2016, https://www .gallup.com/workplace/236453/paycheck-purpose-drives -millennials.aspx.

5. Quoted in Thompson, "Workism," *Atlantic.*

6. Quoted in Thompson, "Workism," *Atlantic.*

7. Anne Helen Petersen, "How Millennials Became the Burnout Generation," *BuzzFeed News*, January 5, 2019, https://www .buzzfeednews.com/article/annehelenpetersen/millennials -burnout-generation-debt-work.

8. Quoted in Thompson, "Workism," *Atlantic.*

9. Ryan Pendell, "Millennials Are Burning Out," Gallup, July 19, 2018, https://www.gallup.com/workplace/237377/millennials -burning.aspx.

10. Rhitu Chatterjee, "Americans Are a Lonely Lot, and Young People Bear the Heaviest Burden," NPR, May 1, 2018, https:// www.npr.org/sections/health-shots/2018/05/01/606588504 /americans-are-a-lonely-lot-and-young-people-bear-the -heaviest-burden.

11. Lila MacLellan, "Millennials Experience Work-Disrupting Anxiety at Twice the US Average Rate," Quartz at Work, December 5, 2018, https://qz.com/work/1483697/millennials -experience-work-disrupting-anxiety-at-twice-the-us-average -rate/.

12. Romans 8.

13. Ephesians 1.

Chapter 1: We're Being Formed, Whether We Like It or Not

1. Gary Chapman, *The Five Love Languages* (Chicago: Northfield, 1992).

2. Alexis C. Madrigal, "When Did TV Watching Peak?" *Atlantic,*

May 30, 2018, https://www.theatlantic.com/technology /archive/2018/05/when-did-tv-watching-peak/561464/.

3. Ralph Jacobson, "2.5 quintillion bytes of data created every day. How does CPG and Retail manage it?" *IBM Industry Insights*, April 24, 2013, https://www.ibm.com/blogs /insights-on-business/consumer-products/2-5-quintillion -bytes-of-data-created-every-day-how-does-cpg-retail -manage-it/.

4. Antonio Regalado, "The Data Made Me Do It," *MIT Technology Review*, May 3, 2013, https://www.technology review.com/s/514346/the-data-made-me-do-it/.

5. M. G. Siegler, "Eric Schmidt: Every 2 Days We Create As Much Information As We Did Up to 2003," *Tech Crunch*, August 4, 2010, https://techcrunch.com/2010/08/04 /schmidt-data/.

6. Bernard Marr, "Big Data: 20 Mind-Boggling Facts Everyone Must Read," *Forbes*, September 30, 2015, https://www.forbes .com/sites/bernardmarr/2015/09/30/big-data-20-mind -boggling-facts-everyone-must-read/#3e00abf017b1.

7. "Data Junkies in Data Junkyard," https://books.google.com /books?id=2bynDgAAQBAJ&pg=PA113&lpg=PA113&dq= data+junkies+living+in+a+data+junkyard&source=bl&ots= jUxldiD02F&sig=ACfU3U35MZ31Y8ovHZ9wF8vOCYoSuE H6dA&hl=en&sa=X&ved=2ahUKEwjt4c-HrKPiAhWDlp4K HXwBAnoQ6AEwA3oECAkQAQ#v=onepage&q=data%20 junkies%20living%20in%20a%20data%20junkyard&f=false entire chapter called data junkies in data junkyard.

8. Google Books Ngram Viewer, https://books.google.com /ngrams/graph?content=goals&year_start=1800&year _end=2000&corpus=15&smoothing=3&share=&direct _url=t1%3B%2Cgoals%3B%2Cc0.

9. This was from Justin Earley. If you haven't read his book *The Common Rule* you need to!

10. Smith has an entire book dedicated to this subject, where the quotes are also from, called *You Are What You Love*.

Chapter 2: This Is Where It Was Always Headed

1. *A Beautiful Mind*, directed by Ron Howard (Universal Studios, 2002), DVD.
2. Gus Lubin, "There's a Staggering Conspiracy Behind the Rise of Consumer Culture," *Business Insider*, February 23, 2013. This is a paraphrase from this article, https://www.business insider.com/birth-of-consumer-culture-2013-2?r=US&IR=T.
3. David Foster Wallace, quoted in Jenna Krajeski, "This Is Water," *New Yorker*, September 19, 2008, https://www .newyorker.com/books/page-turner/this-is-water.
4. "Historical Timeline—Farmers and the Land," https://www .agclassroom.org/gan/timeline/farmers_land.htm.
5. Wendell Berry, "The Agrarian Standard," *Orion Magazine*, https://orionmagazine.org/article/the-agrarian-standard/.
6. Viktor Frankl, *Man's Search for Meaning* (1959; Boston: Beacon, 2006).
7. Olga Fin, "Shabbat Candles in Auschwitz," Chabad.org, accessed May 1, 2019, https://www.chabad.org/library/article _cdo/aid/1457723/jewish/Shabbat-Candles-in-Auschwitz.htm.
8. Warren Farrell and John Gray, *The Boy Crisis* (Dallas: BenBella, 2018).
9. Chip Brown, "The Many Ways Society Makes a Man," *National Geographic*, January 2017, https://www.national geographic.com/magazine/2017/01/how-rites-of-passage -shape-masculinity-gender/.

Chapter 3: Music from Chaos

1. Orison Swett Marden, *Wisdom and Empowerment*, https:// books.google.com/books?id=5HNODwAAQBAJ&pg=PT1028

&lpg=PT1028&dq=orison+marden+"untiring+energy+and
+phenomenal+endurance."&source=bl&ots=arg9KKtuGJ&
sig=ACfU3U3uSfRB0IXnw2rQ4N6uN5C6R0sGyw&hl
=en&sa=X&ved=2ahUKEwjKuajNtKPiAhUIvZ4KHZnNB
jEQ6AEwCXoECAYQAQ#v=onepage&q=orison%20marden
%20"untiring%20energy%20and%20phenomenal%20
endurance."&f=false.

2. Maria Popova, "Thomas Edison, Power-Napper: The Great
Inventor on Sleep and Success," Brainpickings, accessed May
2, 2019, https://www.brainpickings.org/2013/02/11/thomas
-edison-on-sleep-and-success/.

3. Quoted in Popova, "Thomas Edison."

4. Quoted in Popova, "Thomas Edison."

5. Brandon Peters, MD, "What Are the Physical Effects of Sleep
Deprivation on the Human Body?" *VeryWell Health*, March 14,
2019, https://www.verywellhealth.com/what-are-the-physical
-effects-of-sleep-deprivation-3015079. National Institutes of
Health, "Sleep Deprivation Increases Alzheimer's Protein," *NIH
Research Matters*, April 24, 2018, https://www.nih.gov/news
-events/nih-research-matters/sleep-deprivation-increases
-alzheimers-protein. Rachel Cooke, "Sleep Should Be
Prescribed: What Those Late Nights Out Are Costing You,"
Guardian, September 24, 2017, https://www.theguardian.com
/lifeandstyle/2017/sep/24/why-lack-of-sleep-health-worst-enemy
-matthew-walker-why-we-sleep. Seth Maxon, "How Sleep
Deprivation Decays the Mind and Body," *Atlantic*, December
30, 2013, https://www.theatlantic.com/health/archive/2013/12
/how-sleep-deprivation-decays-the-mind-and-body/282395/.

6. Rossie Izlar, "Crop Rotation, Grazing Rebuilds Soil Health,"
American Society of Agronomy, March 7, 2018, https://www
.agronomy.org/science-news/story/crop-rotation-grazing
-rest-promotes-soil-health.

7. C. S. Lewis, *The Magician's Nephew*, 14.

Chapter 4: Why Silence Is So Loud

1. Marco, "Japanese Sensory Gating Study Reveals Profound Cognitive Deficits Present in Chronic Fatigue Syndrome," healthrising.org, July 28, 2013, https://www.healthrising .org/blog/2013/07/28/japanese-sensory-gating-stud-reveals -profound-cognitive-deficits-present-in-chronic-fatigue -syndrome/.

2. L. A. Jones, et al., "Cognitive Mechanisms Associated with Auditory Sensory Gating," *Brain and Cognition* 102 (2016): 33–45, https://www.ncbi.nlm.nih.gov/pmc/articles /PMC4727785/.

3. Cara Buckley, "Working or Playing Indoors, New Yorkers Face an Unabated Roar, *New York Times*, July 19, 2012, https:// www.nytimes.com/2012/07/20/nyregion/in-new-york-city -indoor-noise-goes-unabated.html.

4. Quoted in Buckley, "Working or Playing," *New York Times*.

5. "In New York City Indoor Noise Goes Unabated," *New York Times*, July 20, 2012, https://www.nytimes.com/2012/07/20 /nyregion/in-new-york-city-indoor-noise-goes-unabated.html.

6. Alex Ross, "When Music Is Violence," *New Yorker*, June 27, 2016, https://www.newyorker.com/magazine/2016/07/04/when -music-is-violence.

7. Katherine Bouton, "Silence Is Noisy," *Science Friday*, February 13, 2013, https://www.sciencefriday.com/articles/silence-is-noisy/.

8. Henri Nouwen, *The Essential Henri Nouwen*, ed. Robert A. Jonas (Boston: Shambala, 2009), 100.

9. Nouwen, *Essential*, 100.

10. Henri Nouwen, *The Way of the Heart*, 27–28.

11. Graham Winfrey, "4 Ways Mr. Rogers Forged Deep Relationships with Everyone He Met," https://www.inc.com /graham-winfrey/mr-rogers-documentary-wont-you-be-my -neighbor.html.

12. Elaine Woo, "From the Archives: It's a Sad Day in This Neighborhood," *Los Angeles Times*, February 28, 2003, http://www.latimes.com/local/obituaries/la-me-fred-rogers-20030228-story.html.

13. Quoted in Chris Higgins, "Watch Mister Rogers Accept His Lifetime Achievement Emmy (and Get Ready to Cry at Work)," *Mentalfloss*, May 7, 2018, http://mentalfloss.com/article/27237/mister-rogers-and-his-lifetime-achievement-emmy-get-ready-cry-work.

14. "The Man Trying to Save Silence," https://www.youtube.com/watch?v=jAgCeyW8iTA.

Chapter 5: The Power of No

1. Ian P. Beacock, "A Brief History of (Modern) Time," *Atlantic*, December 22, 2015, https://www.theatlantic.com/technology/archive/2015/12/the-creation-of-modern-time/421419/.

2. Nicolette Jones, "Ruth Belville: The Greenwich Time Lady by David Rooney—review," *Telegraph*, November 26, 2008, https://www.telegraph.co.uk/culture/books/non_fiction reviews/3563649/Ruth-Belville-the-Greenwich-Time-Lady-by-David-Rooney-review.html.

3. Richard Swenson, *Margin: Restoring Emotional, Physical, Financial, and Time Reserves to Overloaded Lives* (Carol Stream: Tyndale, 2004).

4. "Why Do We Overcommit? Study Suggests We Think We'll Have More Time in the Future than We Have Today," *Science Daily*, February 17, 2005, https://www.sciencedaily.com/releases/2005/02/050211084233.htm.

5. David Brooks, "Five Lies Our Culture Tells," *New York Times*, April 15, 2019, https://www.nytimes.com/2019/04/15/opinion/cultural-revolution-meritocracy.html.

6. Jeremy Benstein, "Stop the Machine! The Sabbatical Year

Principle," *My Jewish Learning*, accessed May 6, 2019, https://
www.myjewishlearning.com/article/stop-the-machine-the
-sabbatical-year-principle/.

7. Benstein, "Stop the Machine!" *My Jewish Learning*.

8. Seneca, *On the Brevity of Life* 3.1–2, quoted in Ryan Holiday and
Stephen Hanselman, *The Daily Stoic* (London: Profile, 2016).

Chapter 6: The Desert Gift

1. Jonathan Martin, *Prototype* (Carol Stream: Tyndale, 2013),
back cover.

2. John Mark Comer, "Practices of Silence and Solitude: Jesus
and the Lonely Place," sermon delivered at Bridgetown
Church, Portland, Oregon, January 15, 2017, https://bridge
town.church/series/silence-solitude/.

3. Address by Fred Rogers, Featured Speaker and Honorary
Degree Recipient, 2001, Marquette University, https://www
.marquette.edu/universityhonors/speakers-rogers.shtml.

Chapter 7: A Day of Resistance

1. Steve Crawshaw and John Jackson, "10 Everyday Acts of
Resistance That Changed the World," *Yes Magazine*, updated
November 22, 2016, https://www.yesmagazine.org/people-
power/10-everyday-acts-of-resistance-that-changed-the-world.

2. I talk about this concept much more in detail in my book *It's
Not What You Think*.

3. James Clear, *Atomic Habits* (New York: Random House, 2018),
141–44.

Chapter 8: Empathy

1. Benjamin Franklin, quoted in Sebastian Junger, *Tribe: On
Homecoming and Belonging* (London: HarperCollins UK, 2016), 2–3.

2. Franklin, quoted in Junger, *Tribe*, 2–3.

3. Junger, *Tribe*, 2–3.

4. Junger, *Tribe*, 9.

5. "Thousands of Europeans are Indians and we have no examples of even one of those aborigines having from choice become a European. There must be in their social bond something singularly captivating and far superior to anything to be boasted of among us," lamented the French emigre Hector De Crevecoeur.

6. Steve Kornacki, interviewed by Zoe Chace in *This American Life* episode 662, "Where There Is a Will," https://www.this americanlife.org/662/transcript.

7. This is not to say that politics before Newt were perfect. In fact, the other side of the spectrum had been true for too long; it was a gentleman's club where nothing really got done or anything passionate was talked about much, creating the vacuum for Newt to fill with his new brand of identity politics. Which, by the way, isn't entirely new. Let us never forget Andrew Jackson's incredibly hateful rhetoric or the fact Thomas Jefferson once hired a newspaper journalist to work full time just slandering his opponent John Adams. But it's clear there was a resurgence started in 1979 by Newt, which technology and media and our culture has fanned into a consuming blaze.

8. Andrew Sullivan, "America Wasn't Built for Humans," *New York Magazine*, September 18, 2017, http://nymag.com /intelligencer/2017/09/can-democracy-survive-tribalism.html.

9. Eric Mack, "Forget Dying and Public Speaking: Here's the 47 Things Americans Fear More in 2017," *Inc.com*, October 27, 2017, https://www.inc.com/eric-mack/forget-dying-public -speaking-heres-47-things-americans-fear-more-in-2017.html.

10. Mack, "Forget Dying," *Inc.com*.

11. Psalm 118:6.

12. Quote inspired by: Kosuke Koyama, *Three Mile an Hour God* (SCM Press, 2015), https://www.amazon.com/Three-Mile -Hour-Kosuke-Koyama/dp/0334054214.

Epilogue

1. Adam Chandler, "Why Do Americans Move So Much More than Europeans?" *Atlantic*, October 21, 2016, https://www .theatlantic.com/business/archive/2016/10/us-geographic -mobility/504968/.

ABOUT THE AUTHOR

Jefferson Bethke is the *New York Times* bestselling author of *Jesus > Religion* and *It's Not What You Think*. He and his wife, Alyssa, host *The Real Life Podcast* each week and make YouTube videos that are watched by hundreds of thousands of viewers each month. They also cofounded *Family Teams*, an online initiative that helps families live out God's design by equipping and encouraging them to build a multi-generational team on mission (in all of its different expressions). They live in Maui with their daughter, Kinsley; son, Kannon; new baby girl, Lucy; and dog, Aslan. To say hi or to learn more, go to http://jeffandalyssa.com.